John Edward Lee, C. E Croft

Roman Imperial Profiles

Being a series of more than one hundred and sixty lithographic profiles enlarged

from coins

John Edward Lee, C. E Croft

Roman Imperial Profiles
Being a series of more than one hundred and sixty lithographic profiles enlarged from coins

ISBN/EAN: 9783742833631

Manufactured in Europe, USA, Canada, Australia, Japa

Cover: Foto ©Thomas Meinert / pixelio.de

Manufactured and distributed by brebook publishing software
(www.brebook.com)

John Edward Lee, C. E Croft

Roman Imperial Profiles

ROMAN

IMPERIAL PROFILES

BEING A SERIES OF MORE THAN

One Hundred and Sixty Lithographic Profiles

ENLARGED FROM COINS

ARRANGED BY

JOHN EDWARD LEE, F.S.A., F.G.S.

AUTHOR OF 'ISCA SILURUM'

AND

TRANSLATOR OF KELLER'S 'LAKE DWELLINGS'

LONDON

LONGMANS, GREEN, AND CO.

1874

PREFACE.

A SERIES, nearly complete, of the profiles of the Roman Emperors, Empresses, and Cæsars, has, I believe, never been published in England. Some time since it appeared to me that a work of this kind might be both useful and interesting—useful to coin collectors, especially those who are beginning to study numismatics ; and interesting to the general reader, if he had faith in the accuracy of the pro-files. In order to ensure this accuracy it was necessary not only to have the features drawn correctly from the coins, but also to have an artistic knowledge of the anatomy of the human face ; and I was most happy to be able to secure the co-operation of Mr. C. E. Croft, the well-known artist and portrait-painter of Torquay, who has spared no trouble in producing the following series of excellent profiles. Many of them have been shown to experienced numismatists, and they have expressed them-selves perfectly satisfied with the accuracy of the drawing. I requested Mr. Crofts to copy exactly, and to take no liberties whatever ; and my belief is that he has produced the spirit of the features, in almost every case, in a manner which those who are acquainted with coins will at once be able to appreciate.

The only part of the face in which possibly some license has been taken is the eye. Though the earlier coins are of course in a higher style of art than the later ones, yet even in the earlier coins the eye seems to have been often imperfectly represented, and in the later mints it is drawn quite inaccurately. In the eye, therefore, Mr. Croft has corrected their bad drawing, and this can hardly be called a departure from the original.

It may possibly be thought by those who have not made coins their study, that but little dependence can be placed upon them as likenesses; but this idea may be shown to be groundless by a comparison together of a number of well-executed coins of the same individual, or of the hereditary features which may be traced in the coins of members of the same family. The aid also of well-recognised gems may fairly be called in to give additional faith in the accuracy of numismatic profiles.

With respect to the brief notes on the lives of the Emperors and Empresses, they are almost entirely a translation from Mionnet, and they probably contain all that is necessary in a work of this kind.

A large portion of the coins from which the profiles were drawn are in my own cabinet, but I have been materially helped by several of my friends. The collection of H. Blackmore, Esq. of Torquay, was placed completely at my disposal, and I have to thank him for the loan of many of his best specimens. I have also to return my thanks to the authorities of the British Museum, especially to Percy Gardner, Esq., as I have been enabled to procure from that source impressions of many coins which otherwise would have been out of my reach. I have also to state how much I am indebted to the Rev. S. S. Lewis, of Cambridge, who has materially helped me with the loan of specimens from his collection; and, lastly, I may mention my friend, the Rev. C. W. King, as I have been deeply indebted to him for advice and information, and who, together with the late lamented Mr. Albert Way, decidedly encouraged me to complete the series of profiles. Without the approval of these two well-known antiquaries, it is probable that this work would never have appeared.

No doubt, mistakes will be found out, notwithstanding all the assistance so kindly given to me. I will only add that I have neglected no means in my power of making the collection as complete as possible, and I have done my very best to avoid errors.

VILLA SYRACUSA, TORQUAY:
May 11, 1874.

NOTES

LIVES OF THE ROMAN EMPERORS

ETC.

PLATE I.

POMPEIUS MAGNUS.

ARG.—MAG. PIVS IMP. ITER.

CNÆUS POMPEIUS MAGNUS, the son of Cnæus Pompeius Strabo and Lucilia, was born B.C. 106. In the civil war between Marius and Sylla he took the side of the latter, who, on account of his prowess, gave him the surname of Magnus B.C. 81. He joined with Julius Cæsar and Crassus, and formed with them what is called the first triumvirate B.C. 60. After the death of Crassus, he fell out with Julius Cæsar from the year B.C. 52, and was beaten by him in the battle of Pharsalia in Thessaly, on which he fled to Egypt, and was there put to death B.C. 48 by order of King Ptolemæus.

PLATE II.

JULIUS CÆSAR.

I B.—DIVOS IVLIVS.

Caius Julius Cæsar, the son of Caius Julius Cæsar and Aurelia, was born at Rome B.C. 100. He became one of the triumvirate with Pompeius and Crassus B.C. 60. The following year he was appointed to the government of

Gaul for five years, and this was afterwards renewed to him for another five years. He fell out with Pompeius B.C. 52, and civil war raged between these two rivals B.C. 49. Julius Cæsar gained a decisive victory over Pompeius near Pharsalia B.C. 48, and after this victory he was made dictator for a year. And the dictatorship having been afterwards renewed to him year by year, he was at length made perpetual dictator B.C. 44, but was assassinated shortly afterwards in a full senate by Brutus, Cassius, and other conspirators.

PLATE III.

SEXTUS POMPEIUS.

AUR.—MAG. PIVS IMP. ITER.

Sextus Pompeius, son of Pompeius Magnus, was born B.C. 65. He was defeated in the battle of Munda in Spain B.C. 45. After the death of Julius Cæsar he received from the senate the command of the fleet, with the title of Præfect of the Fleet and the Maritime Shores. Two years afterwards he was proscribed as an accomplice in the death of Julius Cæsar; but notwithstanding this he became master of the sea, and B.C. 39 obliged Marcus Antonius and Octavius to conclude a peace with him, leaving him the possession of Sicily and some other provinces. The following year, however, this peace was broken; and Pompeius, having been defeated in a naval engagement by Octavius, fled into Asia, where he was put to death by order of Marcus Antonius B.C. 35.

This profile is taken from the cast of a coin in the British Museum.

PLATE IV.

BRUTUS.

AUR.—BRVTVS IMP.

Marcus Junius Brutus, the son of Junius Brutus and Servilia the daughter of Cato, was born B.C. 85. He fought under the standard of Pompeius at Pharsalia B.C. 48. He was one of the conspirators in the assassination of Julius Cæsar B.C. 44. Being obliged to leave Rome, he retired with Cassius and the other conspirators to Macedonia, where he was defeated near Philippi by Marcus Antonius and Octavius B.C. 42, and then killed himself.

This profile is taken from the cast of a coin in the British Museum.

PLATE V.

LEPIDUS.

AUR.—M. LEPIDVS III. VIR R.P.C.

Marcus Æmilius Lepidus was born of a patrician family. He took the side of Julius Cæsar against Pompeius, and after the death of Cæsar formed with Octavius and Marcus Antonius the famous triumvirate, taking the title of Triumvir for the Constitution of the Republic B.C. 43. He was deprived of this title by Octavius, and banished to Circeii, a small town of Italy, B.C. 36, where he died in a private station B.C. 13.

The profile is taken from the cast of a gold coin in the British Museum.

PLATE VI.

MARCUS ANTONIUS.

ARG.— M. ANTONIVS IMP. COS. DESIG. ITER. ET TERT.

Marcus Antonius, the son of Marcus Antonius Creticus, was born B.C. 83. He took the side of Julius Cæsar, and helped to defeat Pompeius in the plain of Pharsalia B.C. 48. He became with Lepidus and Octavius a triumvir for the constitution of the republic B.C. 43. Having fallen out with Octavius, he led his troops against him, but was signally defeated near Actium, a town of Acarnania, B.C. 31. After this defeat he was pursued by Octavius to

Egypt, where he killed himself the following year, after having seen both his fleet and his army surrender to his antagonist.

PLATE VII.

OCTAVIA.

AUR.—COS. DESIGN. ITER. ET TER. III. VIR R.P.C.

Octavia was the daughter of Caius Octavius and Atia, and the sister of Octavianus, commonly called Augustus. She was married first to Caius Claudius Marcellus, and after his death to Marcus Antonius B.C. 40. She was divorced from him B.C. 32, and died in the reign of her brother B.C. 10 or 11.

This profile is drawn from the cast of a coin in the British Museum.

PLATE VIII.

CLEOPATRA.

ARG.—CLEOPATRAE REGINAE REGVM FILIORVM REGVM.

Cleopatra, the queen of Egypt, came to the throne by marrying, according to the custom of the country, her own brother Ptolemæus Dionysius B.C. 51. She was divorced some time afterwards by her brother, and was driven from the throne by Pompeius. She was again raised to the throne B.C. 47 by Julius Cæsar, whom she captivated. She also fascinated Marcus Antonius the triumvir after the battle of Philippi B.C. 41, and she received from him the title of Queen of Kings B.C. 34. She joined the forces of this triumvir at the battle of Actium, but was the first to fly into Egypt B.C. 31. She destroyed herself the following year, to avoid being led in triumph by Augustus.

PLATE IX.

AUGUSTUS.

1 B.—CAESAR AVGVSTVS DIVI F. PATER PATRIAE.

Caius Octavius Cæpias, the son of Caius Octavius and Atia, niece of Julius Cæsar, was born at Velletri B.C. 63. He was made by will the heir of his great uncle Julius Cæsar, and was adopted by him, and came to Rome B.C. 44 to receive his inheritance. He then took the names of Caius Julius Cæsar Octavianus. He formed B.C. 43 the league known as the Triumvirate for the Constitution of the Republic, jointly with Marcus Antonius and Lepidus, and, aided by Antonius, defeated at Philippi, in Macedonia, Brutus and Cassius, the murderers of Julius Cæsar, who killed themselves B.C. 42. He also obtained in a naval engagement a decisive victory over Sextus Pompeius B.C. 36, who was put to death by Antonius the following year. Having quarrelled with Antonius he made war with him, and defeated him at the naval battle of Actium B.C. 31 ; and, as Antonius killed himself the following year, Octavius remained the sole master of the republic, which from that time was changed into a monarchy. In the year B.C. 29 Octavius received from the senate the title of Emperor, a title which from that time was used by him as prenomen indicating sovereign power, and which afterwards passed to his successors in the empire. He received from the senate the name of Augustus B.C. 27, by which name he is best known in history, and which has also passed to his successors as a surname. B.C. 2 he was also surnamed the Father of his Country. He died A.D. 14 at Nola, a town of Campania.

PLATES X. and XI.

LIVIA.

PLATE X. 1 B.—As IVSTITIA.
PLATE XI. 2 B.—As PIETAS.

Livia Drusilla, the daughter of Livius Drusus Claudianus, was born B.C. 57. She was married first to Tiberius,

Claudius Nero, from whom she was divorced to marry
Augustus, who on his part divorced his own wife, Scribonia,
B.C. 38.   She died A.D. 29, in the reign of Tiberius, her
son by her first husband.

The features of Livia are recognised in the coins of
1 B. and 2 B., under the characters of Justitia and
Pietas.

The coin from which Plate XI. is drawn is in the collection of H. Blackmore, Esq., of Torquay.

PLATE XII.

AGRIPPA.

2 B.—M. AGRIPPA L. F. COS. III.

Marcus Vipsanius Agrippa, the son-in-law of Augustus,
was born of an obscure family, probably about B.C. 63. He
was a great friend of Augustus from his early years, and
fought under him at Philippi and Actium.   He married
Julia, the daughter of Augustus, after the death of Marcus
Marcellus, her first husband, B.C. 21.   In the year B.C. 18
he received the tribunitial power, and this was continued to
him for five more years.   He died in Campania on his
return from an expedition to Pannonia B.C. 12.

PLATE XIII.

JULIA.

2 B.—N.B. There is no legend on the bronze coin in the British
Museum from which this profile is taken; but the general, if not
universal, opinion is that it represents Julia, the daughter of
Augustus.

Julia, the daughter of Augustus and Scribonia, was born
B.C. 39. She married Marcellus, the son of Octavia, the
sister of Augustus, B.C. 25.   After his death she married
Marcus Agrippa B.C. 21, and after his death she married

Tiberius B.C. 11. On account of her depraved morals Augustus banished her to the island of Pandataria B.C. 2. Ten years later she was taken to Rhegium, in Bruttium, where Tiberius let her die of hunger A.D. 14, a little after he came to the throne.

The coin from which this drawing was taken is in the British Museum.

PLATE XIV.

CAIUS CÆSAR.

AUR.—CAESAR.

Caius Cæsar, the son of M. Agrippa and Julia, was born B.C. 20. He was adopted by Augustus, and made Cæsar B.C. 17. The title of ' Prince of Youth ' was given to him B.C. 5. He died A.D. 4 at Limyra, in Lycia, on his return from an expedition to Armenia.

The profile is taken from the cast of a coin in the British Museum ; and, though the name is not expressly stated on the coin, there can be no doubt as to its referring to Caius Cæsar.

PLATE XV.

TIBERIUS.

2 B.—TI. CAESAR DIVI AUG. F. AVGVST. IMP. VIII.

Tiberius Claudius Nero, the son of Tiberius Claudius Nero and Livia Drusilla, was born B.C. 42. He married, for his first wife, Vipsania Agrippina, the daughter of Marcus Agrippa ; but he divorced her B.C. 11 in order to marry Julia, the daughter of Augustus, and the widow of the same Agrippa. He received B.C. 6 the tribunitial power for five years. He was adopted by Augustus A.D. 4 at the same time as Agrippa Postumus, after the death of Caius and Lucius. From that time he was called Cæsar, and received anew the tribunitial power, which afterwards was given to him year by year. He succeeded Augustus A.D. 14, and then took to himself the surname of Augustus. He died at Misenum, in Campania, put to death by order of Caligula A.D. 37.

PLATE XVI.

DRUSUS (Senr.).

B. Medallion.—NERO CLAVDIVS DRVSVS GERMANICVS IMP.

Nero Claudius Drusus, the brother of Tiberius, was born B.C. 38, and died B.C. 9, in Germany, on his return from his second expedition into that country. The surname of Germanicus was given to him after his death, on account of his victories over the Germans.

The profile is taken from a coin in the collection of Mr. Blackmore.

PLATE XVII.

DRUSUS (Junr.).

1 B.—DRVSVS CAESAR TI. AVG. F. DIVI AVG. N.

Nero Claudius Drusus, the son of Tiberius and Vipsania Agrippina, was born about B.C. 13. He received the tribunitial power A.D. 22. He was poisoned by his wife Livia, or Livilla, A.D. 23.

PLATE XVIII.

ANTONIA.

1 B.—ANTONIA AVGVSTA.

Antonia, the daughter of Marcus Antonius the triumvir, and Octavia, the sister of Augustus, was born B.C. 38 or 39. She became the wife of Drusus, and was poisoned, it is said, by the orders of Caligula, her grandson, A.D. 38.

PLATE XIX.

GERMANICUS.

2 B.—GERMANICVS CAESAR TI. AVGVST. F. DIVI
AVG. N.

Germanicus, the son of Drusus, senr., and Antonia, was born B.C. 15. He was adopted by Tiberius, and made Cæsar A.D. 4. He died at Epidaphne, near Antioch, poisoned by Piso, the governor of Syria, A.D. 19.

PLATE XX.

AGRIPPINA (Senr.).

1 B.—AGRIPPINA M. F. GERMANICI CAESARIS.

Agrippina, the daughter of Agrippa and Julia, and the wife of Germanicus, was born B.C. 15. She was banished by Tiberius A.D. 30 to the island of Pandataria, where he suffered her to die of hunger A.D. 33.

This Agrippina must not be confounded with Vipsania Agrippina, the first wife of Tiberius. She was also the daughter of Agrippa, but by another mother.

PLATE XXI.

CALIGULA.

1 B.—C. CAESAR DIVI AVG. PRON. AVG. P.M.
TR. P. IIII. P.P.

Caius, the son of Germanicus and Agrippina, commonly called Caligula, was born at Antium A.D. 12. He succeeded Tiberius, his great uncle, who had been murdered by his orders A.D. 37. He was assassinated by a tribune of the Prætorian guards A.D. 41.

The profile is taken from a well-preserved coin in Mr. Blackmore's collection.

PLATE XXII.

CLAUDIUS.

1 B.—TI. CLAVDIVS CAESAR AVG. P.M. TR. P. IMP.

Tiberius Claudius Drusus, the son of Drusus, senr. (the brother of Tiberius) and Antonia, was born at Lyons B.C. 10. He was the brother of Germanicus, and uncle to Caligula. On the death of Caligula he was made emperor by the soldiers, and was recognised by the senate A.D. 41. He was poisoned by his wife Agrippina A.D. 54.

PLATE XXIII.

AGRIPPINA (JUNR.),

AUR.—AGRIPP. AVG. DIVI CLAVD. NERONIS CAES. MATER.

Julia Agrippina, the daughter of Germanicus and Agrippina, was born at Cologne A.D. 16. She was the sister of Caligula. She was married first to the senator Cneius Domitius Ahenobarbus A.D. 28, and after his death, which took place A.D. 30, to her uncle, the Emperor Claudius, A.D. 49. She was assassinated by the order of her son Nero A.D. 59.

PLATE XXIV.

BRITANNICUS.

B. MEDALLION.—TI. CLAVDIVS CAESAR AVG. F. BRITANNICVS.

Tiberius Claudius Britannicus, the son of Claudius and Messalina, was born A.D. 42. He was excluded from the throne by the artifices of Agrippina, who made Claudius adopt her son Nero A.D. 50. Britannicus was poisoned by order of Nero A.D. 55.

PLATE XXV.

NERO.

1 B.—NERO CLAVD. CAESAR AVG. GER. P.M. TR. P. IMP. P.P.

Lucius Domitius Nero, the son of Cneius Domitius Ahenobarbus and Agrippina, junr., was born at Antium A.D. 37. He was adopted by Claudius, and made Cæsar A.D. 50, when he took the names of Tiberius Claudius Nero Drusus. He received the title of 'Prince of Youth' A.D. 51. He succeeded Claudius A.D. 54. On the revolt of Galba and his elevation to the empire, Nero destroyed himself A.D. 68.

PLATE XXVI.

POPPÆA.

'POTIN.'—ΠΟΠΠ(ΑΙΑ ΝΕΡΩΝΟ)Σ Σ(ΕΒΑΣΤΟΥ).

Poppæa Sabina, the daughter of Titus Ollius, and grand-daughter of Poppæus Sabinus, a man of consular dignity, was the second wife of Nero, and was married to him A.D. 63. She died from a kick given to her by Nero A.D. 66.

The coin from which this profile was taken is in the collection of Mr. Blackmore.

PLATE XXVII.

CLODIUS MACER.

ARG.—CLODIVS MACER.

Lucius Clodius Macer was legate in Africa under Nero, and on the news of his death and the revolt of Galba, A.D. 68, he incited the legions of that province to revolt, and prepared to seize the sovereign power, but was over-come and put to death the same year by one of Galba's lieutenants.

The profile is taken from a coin in the British Museum.

PLATE XXVIII.

GALBA.

1 B.—SER. GALBA IMP. CAES. AVG. TR. P.

Servius Sulpicius Galba was born of an illustrious family B.C. 3. He was the governor of Tarragonese Spain, under Nero, when he revolted against him at the instigation of Vindex, the governor of Gaul, and he was proclaimed emperor in both provinces. He was acknowledged also by the senate and the Prætorian soldiers, and succeeded Nero who had killed himself A.D. 68. The following year, after a reign of seven months, Galba was killed by the Prætorian soldiers, who proclaimed Otho in his stead.

PLATE XXIX.

OTHO.

AUR.—IMP. OTHO CAESAR AVG. TR. P.

Marcus Salvius Otho, the son of Lucius Salvius Otho and Albia Terentia, was born of illustrious parentage A.D. 32. When governor of Lusitania under Nero he joined the revolt of Galba A.D. 68. The following year he conspired against Galba, and had him assassinated by the Prætorian soldiers, who proclaimed him emperor. He was, however, obliged to contend for the empire with Vitellius, who had been chosen emperor by the legions of Germany ; and having been defeated he killed himself the same year, A.D. 69, having only reigned ninety-five days.

PLATE XXX.

VITELLIUS.

1 B.—A. VITELLIVS GERMAN. IMP. AVG. P.M. TR. P.

Aulus Vitellius, the son of Lucius Vitellius and Sextilia, was born A.D. 15. He was sent by Galba as legate into

Lower Germany A.D. 68. The following year he was proclaimed emperor by the legions of Germany, who had revolted against Galba at the time that Otho was acknowledged as emperor by the Prætorian cohorts at Rome. Vitellius maintained himself on the throne by defeating Otho in battle, who afterwards killed himself. But Vitellius was put to death the same year, A.D. 69, after a short reign of eight months, by the soldiers, who took the side of Vespasianus, and who had become masters of Rome.

The profile is taken from a coin in the collection of Mr. Blackmore.

PLATE XXXI.

VESPASIANUS.

1 B.—IMP. CAES. AVG. VESPAS. COS. II. TR. POT.

Flavius Vespasianus, the son of Flavius Sabinus and Vespasia Polla, was born near Reate, in the Sabine country, A.D. 9. He was sent by Nero to pacify Judæa and to be the governor there A.D. 66. He was proclaimed emperor by the legions of Egypt ; and having been recognised successively by those of Judæa and Syria, and also by those of Mæsia and Pannonia, they marched to Rome, and, having taken possession of it, they put Vitellius to death. Vespasianus consequently remained sole master of the empire A.D. 69. He died at Reate A.D. 79.

PLATE XXXII.

DOMITILLA.

ARG.—DIVA DOMITILLA AVGVSTA.

Flavia Domitilla, the daughter of Flavius Liberalis, said to have been a Quæstorian notary or clerk, was married to Vespasianus about A.D. 40. She died before he became emperor.

PLATE XXXIII.

TITUS.

1 B.—IMP. T. CAES. VESP. AVG. P.M. TR. P.P. P. COS. VIII.

Titus Flavius Vespasianus, the son of Vespasianus and Domitilla, was born at Rome A.D. 41. His father made him Cæsar and 'Prince of Youth' A.D. 69, and A.D. 71 he was made emperor and associated in the sovereign power. On his father's death A.D. 79 he became sole emperor. He died A.D. 81. His name is well known in history in connection with the siege of Jerusalem.

PLATE XXXIV.

JULIA (Titi).

1 B.—IVLIA IMP. T. AVG. F. AVGVSTA.

Julia, the daughter of Titus and Marcia Furnilla, was married to Flavius Sabinus, the son of Titus Flavius Sabinus, the brother of Vespasianus. She died in the reign of her uncle Domitianus.

The profile is from the sulphur cast of a 1 B. in Mr. Blackmore's collection.

PLATE XXXV.

DOMITIANUS.

1 B.—IMP. CAES. DOMIT. AVG. GERM. COS. XIIII. CENS. PER. P.P.

Domitianus, the brother of Titus, was born A.D. 51. He became Cæsar and 'Prince of Youth' at the same time as his brother A.D. 69. He succeeded Titus A.D. 81, and was assassinated by a freedman A.D. 96.

PLATE XXXVI.

DOMITIA.

1 B.—DOMITIA AVG. IMP. CAES. DIVI F. DOMITIAN. AVG.

Domitia Longina, the daughter of Cneius Domitius Corbulo, a man of consular dignity, was first married to the senator Lucius Lamia Æmilianus ; but she was taken away from him by Domitianus, who married her A.D. 70. She died in the reign of Trajanus.

PLATE XXXVII.

NERVA.

1 B.—IMP. NERVA CAES. AVG. P.M. TR. P. COS. II. P.P.

Marcus Cocceius Nerva was born at Narnia, a town of Umbria, of a family of consular dignity A.D. 32. After having been prætor and twice consul, he was chosen emperor by the senate and the Prætorian soldiers the day on which Domitian died A.D. 96. Nerva died A.D. 98.

PLATE XXXVIII.

TRAJANUS.

1 B.—IMP. NERVAE TRAJANO AVG. GER. DAC. P.M. TR. P. COS. V. P.P.

Marcus Ulpius Trajanus Crinitus was born at Italica, in Spain, A.D. 53. He was the governor of Lower Germany under Domitianus and Nerva. He was adopted by Nerva, and associated in the empire with the titles of Cæsar and Imperator, but without that of Augustus, A.D. 97. He succeeded Nerva A.D. 98, and then took the title of Augustus. He died at Selinunte, in Cilicia, A.D. 117.

PLATE XXXIX.

PLOTINA.

1 B.—PLOTINA AVG. IMP. TRAJANI.

Pompeia Plotina was married to Trajanus long before he came to the throne. She died A.D. 129 in the reign of Hadrianus.

PLATE XL.

MARCIANA.

1 B.—DIVA AVGVSTA MARCIANA.

Marciana was the sister of Trajanus. She died about A.D. 114.

PLATE XLI.

MATIDIA.

1 B.—MATIDIA AVG. DIVAE MARCIANAE F.

Matidia was the daughter of Marciana, and mother-in-law of Hadrianus. She died, it is believed, in the reign of Antoninus.

This profile is drawn from the sulphur cast of a 1 B. in the collection of Mr. Blackmore.

PLATE XLII.

HADRIANUS.

1 B.—HADRIANVS AVG. COS. III. P.P.

Publius Ælius Hadrianus, the son of Ælius Hadrianus Afer and Domitia Paulina, was the cousin of Trajanus and the son-in-law of Matidia. He was born at Rome, or, according to other accounts, at Italica in Spain, A.D. 76. He was adopted by Trajanus shortly before his death

A.D. 117, and then succeeded to the throne.   Hadrianus died at Baiæ, in Campania, A.D. 138.

PLATE XLIII.

SABINA.

1 B.—SABINA AVGVSTA HADRIANI AVG. P.P.

Julia Sabina was the daughter of Matidia, and was married to Hadrianus about A.D. 100.   She destroyed herself A.D. 137.

This profile is from a sulphur cast in the collection of Mr. Blackmore.

PLATE XLIV.

ÆLIUS CÆSAR.

AUR.—L. AELIVS CAESAR.

Lucius Aurelius Cejonius Commodus Verus, the son of Cejonius Commodus, a man of consular dignity, was adopted by Hadrianus A.D. 135 or 136, when he was made Cæsar, and took the names of Lucius Ælius Verus.   He died A.D. 138.

PLATE XLV.

ANTINOUS.

B. MEDALLION.—ANTINOOY HPΩOC.

This favourite of Hadrianus was born in Bithynia, and died A.D. 130.

PLATE XLVI.

ANTONINUS PIUS.

B. MEDALLION.—IMP. T. AEL. CAES. HADR. ANTONINVS AVG. PIVS.

Titus Aurelius Fulvius Bojonius Arrius Antoninus, the son of Aurelius Fulvius, a man of consular dignity, and

Arria Fadilla, was born at Lanuvium, a town of Latium, A.D. 86. After the death of Ælius he was adopted by Hadrianus, and received the title of Cæsar and the tribunitial power A.D. 138. He then took the names of T. Ælius Hadrianus Antoninus. He succeeded Hadrian the same year, and received from the senate the title of Augustus and the surname of Pius. A.D. 139 he took the title of Pater Patriæ. He died at Lorium, in Etruria, A.D. 161.

PLATE XLVII.

FAUSTINA (Senr.).

B. Medallion.—DIVA AVG. FAVSTINA.

Annia Galeria Faustina, the daughter of Annius Verus, præfect of the city, was born A.D. 105. She married Antoninus before his adoption by Hadrianus. She died A.D. 141.

The medallion from which this sketch was taken is in the possession of the Rev. S. S. Lewis, of Cambridge.

PLATES XLVIII. and XLIX.

MARCUS AURELIUS.

Plate XLVIII.—As CÆSAR.

1 B.—AVRELIVS CAESAR AVG. PII F.

Plate XLIX—As EMPEROR.

1. B.—M. AVREL. ANTONINVS AVG. P.M.

Marcus Annius Verus Catillus Severus, the son of Annius Verus, the prætor, and Domitia Calvilla, was born at Rome A.D. 121. He was named by Hadrianus M. Annius Verissimus after the death of his father. He was adopted by Antoninus at the time when Antoninus was adopted by Hadrianus, A.D. 138, when he was made Cæsar,

and from that time was called M. Ælius Aurelius Verus.
He received the tribunitial power A.D. 147. He succeeded
Antoninus A.D. 161, and then took the names of Marcus
Aurelius Antoninus. He died at Vindobona, in Pannonia,
A.D. 180.

The profile drawn Plate XLVIII. is from a coin in Mr.
Blackmore's collection.

PLATE L.

FAUSTINA (JUNR.).

B. MEDALLION.—FAVSTINA AVG. PII AVG. FIL.

Annia Faustina, the daughter of Antoninus Pius and
Galeria Faustina, was married to Marcus Aurelius about
A.D. 140. She died A.D. 175.

PLATE LI.

ANNIUS VERUS.

B. MEDALLION.—VERVS CAES.

Annius Verus, the son of Marcus Aurelius and Faustina,
junr., was born A.D. 163. He was made Cæsar A.D. 166, and
died at Præneste, a town of Latium, A.D. 170.

This profile is taken from a coin in the British
Museum, which gives the likeness both of Commodus and
Verus.

PLATE LII.

LUCIUS VERUS.

1 B.—IMP. CAES. L. AVREL. VERVS AVG.

Lucius Cejonius Commodus, the son of Ælius Cæsar
and son-in-law of Aurelius, was born at Rome A.D. 130.
After the adoption of his father by Hadrianus, A.D. 135, he
was called L. Cejonius Ælius Aurelius Commodus. He

was adopted by Antoninus at the same time as Marcus Aurelius, A.D. 138, but without the title of Cæsar. After the death of Antoninus, A.D. 161, he was associated in the empire by Marcus Aurelius, when he took at once the titles of Cæsar and Augustus, and was then called Lucius Ælius Aurelius Verus. He died at Altinum, in Venetia, poisoned, it is said, by his wife Lucilla, A.D. 169.

PLATE LIII.

LUCILLA.

B. MEDALLION.—LVCILLAE AVG. ANTONINI AVG. F.

Annia Lucilla, the daughter of Marcus Aurelius and Faustina, junr., was born A.D. 147. She married Lucius Verus A.D. 164, and afterwards, A.D. 170, Claudius Pompeius, a Roman senator. She joined in a conspiracy against Commodus A.D. 183, and was banished to the island of Capreæ, where she was put to death shortly afterwards.

PLATE LIV.

COMMODUS.

B. MEDALLION.—IMP. COMMODVS AVG. PIVS FELIX.

Lucius or Marcus Ælius Aurelius Commodus Antoninus, the son of Marcus Aurelius and Faustina, junr., was born at Lanuvium, a town of Latium, A.D. 161. He was made Cæsar A.D. 166, at the same time as his brother Annius Verus. He was made 'Prince of Youth' A.D. 175. He was associated in the empire with the title of Imperator, but without that of Augustus, A.D. 176 ; and at the same time he received the tribunitial power. He received the title of Augustus A.D. 177, and succeeded his father A.D. 180. He was put to death, A.D. 192, by one of the companions of his debaucheries.

PLATE LV.

CRISPINA.

1 B.—CRISPINA AVGVSTA.

Bruttia Crespina, the daughter of Bruttius Præsens, a senator, was married to Commodus A.D. 177, and, on account of her irregularities, was banished to the island of Capreæ, where she was put to death about A.D. 183.

PLATE LVI.

PERTINAX.

1 B.—IMP. CAES. P. HELV. PERTINAX AVG.

Publius Helvius Pertinax, the son of Helvius Successus, a freedman, was born at Alba Pompeia, or, according to other accounts, at Villa Martis, in Liguria, A.D. 126. He was præfect of Rome under Commodus, and, after the death of this prince, he was chosen emperor by the Prætorian soldiers and the senate A.D. 192. But he was assassinated the year following by the very same band of soldiers who had raised him to the throne. He reigned only eighty-seven days.

PLATE LVII.

TITIANA.

SILVER MEDALLION.—ΘΕΑ TITIANA.

Flavia Titiana, the daughter of Flavius Sulpicianus, a senator and præfect of the city, was the wife of Pertinax. Very little is known respecting her. When her husband died she retired into private life.

The profile is taken from a rare coin in Mr. Blackmore's collection.

PLATE LVIII.

DIDIUS JULIANUS.

1 B.—IMP. CAES. M. DID. SEVER. IVLIAN. AVG.

Marcus Didius Severus Julianus, the son of Petronius Didius Severus and Clara Æmilia, was born at Milan A.D. 133. He was governor of Africa under Commodus, and 'Præfectus vigilum' under Pertinax. On the death of the latter prince the empire was put up for sale by the Prætorian soldiers, and Didius Julianus, having offered the largest sum, was proclaimed emperor A.D. 193; but on the news of the approach of Severus, who had been chosen emperor by the legions of Pannonia, Didius was put to death by order of the senate the same year, having reigned only sixty-six days.

PLATE LIX.

MANLIA SCANTILLA.

1 B.—MANLIA SCANTILLA AVG.

Manlia Scantilla, the wife of Didius Julianus, retired into private life after the death of her husband.

PLATE LX.

DIDIA CLARA.

1 B.—DIDIA CLARA AVG.

Didia Clara, the daughter of Didius Julianus and Manlia Scantilla, was born about A.D. 153. She married the senator Cornelius Repentinus, præfect of Rome under Julianus.

PLATE LXI.

PESCENNIUS NIGER.

1 B.—ΑΥΤ. Κ. ΠΕCΚ. ΝΙΓΡΟC ΙΟΥCΤΟC CΕΒ.

Caius Pescennius Niger, the son of Annius Fuscus and Lampridia, was the governor of Syria and general of the legions of Asia under Commodus and Pertinax. He was proclaimed emperor by his troops at Antioch on the news of the death of Pertinax, and shortly after the elevation of Didius Julianus to the throne of Rome A.D. 193. He was vanquished in several battles with Severus, and was killed by his soldiers the following year, having only reigned about twelve months.

The coin from which this profile was taken is in Mr. Blackmore's collection.

PLATE LXII.

CLODIUS ALBINUS.

1 B.—D. CLOD. SEPT. ALBIN. CAES.

Decimus Clodius Septimius Albinus, the son of Cejonius Postumus and Aurelia Messalina, was born at Hadrumetum, in Africa, of a noble family. He was the governor of Britain under Commodus and Pertinax. He was proclaimed emperor by his legions A.D. 193; nearly at the time that Pescennius Niger was proclaimed in opposition to Didius Julianus by the legions of Syria, and Severus by those of Pannonia. Clodius was satisfied with the title of Cæsar, which Severus gave to him to attach him to his interests. But after the death of Pescennius, Clodius found himself neglected by Severus, who would not grant him even the title of Cæsar, and, it is said, had some designs against his life. He consequently revolted against Severus, took the title of Augustus, and led his army into Gaul A.D. 196. He was, however, killed the following year in a bloody battle with Severus near Lyons.

PLATE LXIII.
SEVERUS.
1 B.—SEVERVS PIVS AVG. P. M. TR. P. XII.

Lucius Septimius Severus, the son of Marcus Septimius Geta, a senator, and Fulvia Pia, was born at Leptis, in Africa, A.D. 146. He was governor of Pannonia and Illyria under Commodus and Pertinax. After the death of the latter he was proclaimed emperor by the legions of these provinces, and marched to Rome, where he was recognised by the senate, who put Didius Julianus to death A.D. 193. Severus then added to his other names that of Pertinax. After he had successively got rid of his rivals, Pescennius Niger and Clodius Albinus, he remained sole master of the empire A.D. 197. He died at York A.D. 211.

PLATE LXIV.
JULIA DOMNA.
1 B.—DIVA IVLIA AVGVSTA.

Julia Domna, the daughter of Bassianus, of a plebeian family, was born at Emesa, in Syria, and was married to Severus A.D. 173. She starved herself to death after the assassination of her son Caracalla.

PLATE LXV.
CARACALLA.
B. MEDALLION.—M. AVRELIVS ANTONINVS PIVS AVG. BRIT. PM. TR. P. XVI.

Bassianus (commonly called Caracalla), the son of Septimius Severus and Julia Domna, was born at Lyons A.D. 188. He was made Cæsar by his father A.D. 196, and then took the names of Marcus Aurelius Antoninus. He received the title of Augustus and the tribunitial power A.D. 198. He succeeded his father A.D. 211, jointly with his brother Geta, but the following year he had him assassinated in the arms of his mother. Caracalla was assassinated A.D. 217, at the instigation of Macrinus, the Prætorian præfect, as he was preparing for an expedition against Parthia.

PLATE LXVI.

PLAUTILLA.

AUR.—PLAVTILLAE AVGVSTAE.

Fulvia Plautilla, the daughter of Plautianus the Prætorian præfect, was married to Caracalla A.D. 202. The following year she was banished by her husband either to Sicily or Lipari, where she was put to death, A.D. 212, by the orders of Caracalla.

PLATE LXVII.

GETA.

1 B.—P. SEPTIMIVS GETA CAES.

Lucius or Publius Septimius Geta, the brother of Caracalla, was born at Milan about A.D. 189. He was made Cæsar A.D. 198, at the time when Caracalla was made Augustus. In the year A.D. 209 he was made Augustus by his father and received the tribunitial power. He succeeded to the empire jointly with his brother A.D. 211, but was assassinated by his directions, the following year, in the arms of their mother. Geta only reigned thirteen months.

PLATE LXVIII.

MACRINUS.

1 B.—IMP. CAES. M. OPEL. SEV. MACRINVS AVG.

Marcus Opelius Severus Macrinus was born at Cæsarea, in Mauritania, of obscure parentage, A.D. 164. He was the Prætorian præfect under Caracalla, and, finding that this prince had designs upon his life, he had him assassinated, and was himself proclaimed emperor by the army, A.D. 217. He was, however, killed the following year, after having been defeated by Elagabalus, who had been chosen emperor by the army of Syria. Macrinus reigned only fourteen months.

PLATE LXIX.

DIADUMENIANUS.

1 B.—M. OPEL. ANTONINVS DIADVMENIANVS CAES.

Marcus Opelius Diadumenianus, the son of Macrinus and Nonia Celsa, was born A.D. 208. He was made Cæsar by his father A.D. 217, when he received the additional name of Antoninus. He was called Augustus also the same year. He was killed shortly after his father by the soldiers of Elagabalus A.D. 218.

PLATE LXX.

ELAGABALUS.

ARG.—IMP. ANTONINVS PIVS AVG.

Varius Avitus Bassianus, the son of Sextus Varius Marcellus and Julia Soæmias, the niece of Julia Domna, was born at Emesa, in Syria, A.D. 205. In this place there was a temple to Elagabalum or the sun, and Bassianus, with his cousin Alexianus, became, while yet young, priests of this divinity—hence arose his name Elagabalus. He was proclaimed emperor by the legions of Syria A.D. 218, when he took the names of Marcus Aurelius Antoninus. By the death of Macrinus and his son Diadumenianus, Elagabalus remained sole master of the empire. He was put to death at Rome, A.D. 222, by the Prætorian soldiers, who were indignant at his conduct to his cousin, Alexander Severus, whom he wished to destroy, although he had adopted him and made him Cæsar only a few months previously.

·PLATE LXXI.

JULIA PAULA.

1 B.—IVLIA PAVLA AVG.

Julia Cornelia Paula, the daughter of Julius Paulus, the Prætorian præfect, was married to Elagabalus A.D. 219, but was divorced by him at the end of a year, and then retired into private life.

The profile is drawn from the sulphur cast of a 1 B. in Mr. Blackmore's collection.

PLATE LXXII.

AQUILIA SEVERA.

ARG.—IVLIA AQVILIA SEVERA AVG.

Julia Aquilia Severa, the daughter of Quintus Aquilius Sabinus, a man of consular dignity, was the second wife of Elagabalus; and, though a vestal virgin, was married to him A.D. 220. She was divorced soon afterwards; but in process of time, after Elagabalus had had other wives, and dismissed them, Aquilia Severa was recalled, and remained with him till his death A.D. 222.

PLATE LXXIII.

ANNIA FAUSTINA.

2 B.—ANNIA FAVSTINA AVGVSTA.

Annia Faustina, the daughter of the senator Claudius Severus and Vibia Aurelia Sabina, who was the daughter of Marcus Aurelius and Faustina, junr., was the third wife of Elagabalus, and was married to him A.D. 221, but was divorced almost immediately to make way for others.

PLATE LXXIV.

JULIA SOÆMIAS.

2 B.—IVL. SOAEMIAS AVG.

Julia Soæmias, the daughter of Julius Avitus, a man of consular dignity, and Julia Mæsa, the sister of Julia Domna, was the mother of Elagabalus, and was killed by the Prætorian soldiers at the same time as her son A.D. 222.

From Mr. Blackmore's collection.

PLATE LXXV.

JULIA MÆSA.

2 B.—IVLIA MAESA AVGVSTA.

Julia Mæsa, the sister of Julia Domna, and grandmother of Elagabalus, died in the reign of Alexander Severus A.D. 223.

PLATE LXXVI.

SEVERUS ALEXANDER.

1 B.—IMP. ALEXANDER PIVS AVG.

Bassianus Alexianus, the son of Gessius Marcianus and Julia Mamæa, the sister of Julia Soæmias, was born at Arca, in Phœnicia, A.D. 205. He was adopted by Elagabalus, and made Cæsar A.D. 221, when he took the names of Marcus Aurelius Alexander. After the death of Elagabalus he was made Augustus and emperor by the senate A.D. 222, when he added Severus to his other names. He was assassinated near Mayence by some soldiers, instigated, it is said, by Maximinus, one of his generals, A.D. 235.

PLATE LXXVII.
ORBIANA.
1 B.—SALL. BARBIA ORBIANA AVG.

Sallustia Barbia Orbiana was the third wife of Severus Alexander, but is only known by her coins. From a medal struck at Alexandria it appears that she was his wife in the fifth year of his reign, viz. A.D. 226.

PLATE LXXVIII.
JULIA MAMÆA.
1 B.—IVLIA MAMAEA AVGVSTA.

Julia Mamæa, the sister of Soæmias, and the mother of Severus Alexander, was assassinated at the same time as her son A.D. 235.

PLATE LXXIX.
MAXIMINUS.
1 B.—IMP. MAXIMINVS PIVS AVG.

Caius Julius Verus Maximinus was born in Thrace of obscure parentage. He was general under Severus Alexander, who was assassinated by his orders when on an expedition to Germany. Maximinus was proclaimed emperor in his stead by the soldiers A.D. 235. Maximinus was himself assassinated by the soldiers before Aquileia A.D. 238.

PLATE LXXX.
PAULINA.
1 B.—DIVA PAVLINA.

There is considerable doubt as to the right appropriation of this coin ; but the general opinion is, that Paulina was the wife of the Emperor Maximinus. She is, however, only known by her coins.

PLATE LXXXI.

MAXIMUS CÆSAR.

1 B.—C. IVL. VERVS MAXIMVS CAES.

Caius Julius Verus Maximus, the son of Maximinus
and probably of Paulina, was made Cæsar by his father
A.D. 235.   He was killed at the same time as Maximinus.

PLATE LXXXII.

GORDIANUS AFRICANUS (Senr.).

1 B.—IMP. CAES. M. ANT. GORDIANVS AFR. AVG.

Marcus Antonius Gordianus (commonly called Gordianus Africanus the elder), the son of Metius Marullus
and Ulpia Gordiana, was born at Rome, of illustrious
parentage, about A.D. 158.   He was proconsul of Africa
under Severus Alexander and Maximinus from the year
230 A.D.   He was proclaimed emperor by the legions of
this province, and acknowledged by the senate, who declared Maximinus the enemy of his country A.D. 238.   He
killed himself the same year, after having reigned only
about forty-five days, on hearing of the loss of a battle
between his son and Capellienus, the lieutenant of Maximinus, in Mauritania, in which his son was killed.

The profile is taken from the sulphur cast of a 1 B. in
Mr. Blackmore's collection.

PLATE LXXXIII.

GORDIANUS AFRICANUS (Junr.).

1 B.—IMP. CAES. M. ANT. GORDIANVS AFR. AVG.

Marcus Antonius Gordianus, the son of Gordianus
Africanus, senr., and Fabia Orestilla (commonly called
Gordianus Africanus II. or junr.), was born A.D. 192.   He

was sent with his father to Africa as legate or lieutenant A.D. 230. He was named emperor jointly with his father A.D. 238, but was killed a few weeks afterwards in a battle with Capellienus, the lieutenant of Maximinus, in Mauritania.

PLATE LXXXIV.

BALBINUS.

1 B.—IMP. CAES. D. CAEL. BALBINVS AVG.

Decimus Cælius Balbinus was born, about A.D. 178, of an illustrious family. He was chosen emperor by the senate jointly with Pupienus, after the death of the two Gordians, A.D. 238, in opposition to Maximinus, who was assassinated shortly afterwards. Balbinus, however, with his colleague, was put to death in three months by the Prætorian soldiers, who were indignant that these two emperors should have been chosen without their consent.

PLATE LXXXV.

PUPIENUS.

1 B.—IMP. CAES M. CLOD. PVPIENVS AVG.

Marcus Clodius Pupienus Maximus was born, A.D. 164, of low origin. He was made Augustus by the senate with Balbinus A.D. 238, and killed with him in about three months by the Prætorian soldiers.

PLATE LXXXVI.

GORDIANUS PIUS.

B. MEDALLION.—IMP. GORDIANVS_PIVS FELIX AVG.

Marcus Antonius Gordianus, the son of Gordianus, junr., was born about A.D. 222. He is commonly called Gordianus Pius, or Gordianus III. He was made Cæsar by the senate when Balbinus and Pupienus were elevated

to the empire A.D. 238; and after their death, in the same
year, he was proclaimed Augustus. He was assassinated,
A.D. 244, at the instigation of Philip, the Prætorian præfect.

PLATE LXXXVII.

TRANQUILLINA.

ARG.—SABINIA TRANQVILLINA AVG.

Furia Sabinia Tranquillina, the daughter of Misitheus,
the Prætorian præfect, was married to Gordianus Pius A.D.
241. It is not known what became of her after the death
of her husband.

The coin from which this profile was taken is in Mr.
Blackmore's collection.

PLATE LXXXVIII.

PHILIPPUS (Senr.).

1 B.—IMP. M. IVL. PHILIPPVS AVG.

Marcus Julius Philippus was born at Bostra, in Arabia,
A.D. 204. He was made Prætorian præfect by Gordianus
Pius after the death of Misitheus, father-in-law to Gordianus,
A.D. 243. He was proclaimed emperor the following year
by the Prætorian soldiers after the death of Gordianus, who
had been assassinated by his orders. He was killed near
Verona, A.D. 249, after a defeat by Trajanus Decius, who
had been chosen emperor by the legions of Pannonia.

PLATE LXXXIX.

OTACILIA.

1 B.—MARCIA OTACIL. SEVERA AVG.

Marcia Otacilia Severa was married to Philippus, about
A.D. 234, before he came to the throne. She retired into
private life after the death of her husband.

PLATE XC.

PHILIPPUS (JUNR.).

1 B.—M. IVL. PHILIPPVS NOBIL. CAESAR.

Marcus Julius Philippus, the son of Philippus, senr., and Otacilia, was born about A.D. 237. He was made Cæsar by his father A.D. 244. He was associated in the empire with the title of Augustus A.D. 247. He was killed by the Prætorian soldiers shortly after the death of his father A.D. 249.

PLATE XCI.

TRAJANUS DECIUS.

B. MEDALLION.—IMP. C.M.Q. TRAJANVS DECIVS·AVG.

Caius Messius Quintus Trajanus Decius was born at Bubalia, near Sirmium, in Pannonia, A.D. 201. He was sent by Philip to quell the revolt of Marinus in Mœsia and Pannonia, but was himself chosen emperor by the legions of these provinces, and kept his position by the death of Philip, whom he defeated. He lost his life in a marsh, so that his body was never found, after having been defeated by the Goths near Abricium, in Thrace.

A numismatic friend has objected to the smooth face here given of Trajanus Decius, as he ought to have had a beard. The coin, however, was copied accurately, and as the features seem very characteristic I have ventured on retaining it ; but I will give my friend's objection in his own words. 'The explanation seems to be : The close-cropped beard, "ad pectinem tonsa," then in fashion, has disappeared through the wear of the coin from which the portrait was taken.'

PLATE XCII.

ETRUSCILLA.

1 B.—HERENNIA ETRVSCILLA AVG.

Herennia Etruscilla was the wife of Trajanus Decius, but is known only by her coins and by one inscription.

D

PLATE XCIII.

HERENNIUS ETRUSCUS.

ARG.—Q. HER. ETR. MES. DECIVS NOB. C.

Quintus Herennius Etruscus Messius Trajanus Decius, the son of Trajanus Decius and Etruscilla, was made Cæsar by his father A.D. 249, and Augustus A.D. 251. He was killed that year in the battle in which his father lost his life.

PLATE XCIV.

HOSTILIANUS.

1 B.—C. VALENS HOSTIL. MES. QVINTVS N.C.

Caius Valens Hostilianus Messius Quintus, also the son of Trajanus Decius and Etruscilla, was made Cæsar at the same time as his brother Herennius A.D. 249. He was adopted and associated in the empire with the title of Augustus by Trebonianus, the successor of Trajanus Decius, A.D. 251 ; but he died some months afterwards, in the same year, of the plague ; or, according to other accounts, secretly poisoned by Trebonianus.

This profile is from a coin in Mr. Blackmore's collection.

PLATE XCV.

TREBONIANUS GALLUS.

1 B.—IMP.CAES.C.VIBIVS TREBONIANVS GALLVS AVG.

Caius Vibius Trebonianus Gallus was born in the island of Meninx, on the coast of Africa, about A.D. 207. When general of the Roman army he was proclaimed emperor by the legions after the death of Trajanus Decius A.D. 251, but he was killed by his own soldiers, near Interamnum (Terni), when he was leading them against Æmilianus, who had been chosen emperor by the legions of Mœsia, A.D. 254.

PLATE XCVI.

VOLUSIANUS.

ARG.—IMP. CAE. C. VIB. VOLVSIANO AVG.

Caius Vibius Afinius Trebonianus Gallus Veldumnianus Volusianus, the son of Trebonianus, was made Cæsar by his father A.D. 251.   After the death of Hostilianus he was named Augustus and associated in the empire A.D. 252. He was assassinated by the soldiers at the same time as his father A.D. 254.

PLATE XCVII.

ÆMILIANUS.

3 B. PLATED.—IMP. AEMILIANVS PIVS FEL. AVG.

Marcus or Caius Julius Æmilius Æmilianus was born of an obscure family in Mauritania about A.D. 208. He was governor of Mœsia and Pannonia under Trebonianus.   He was proclaimed emperor by the legions of these provinces A.D. 253, and kept in this position by the death of Trebonianus, which happened the following year.   He was killed after a reign of three months by his own soldiers, near Spoletta, in Umbria, as he was preparing to dispute the empire with Valerianus, who had been chosen emperor by the legions of Rhætia and Noricum A.D. 254.

PLATES XCVIII. AND XCVIII. No. 2.

VALERIANUS.

PL. XCVIII.

3 B. PLATED.—VALERIANVS P.F. AVG.

PL. XCVIII. No. 2.

1 B.—IMP. C.P. LIC. VALERIANVS P.F. AVG.

Publius Licinius Valerianus was born of an illustrious family A.D. 190. He was ordered by Trebonianus to march against Æmilianus, who had been chosen emperor by the legions of Mœsia, and he collected an army in Rhætia and Noricum, but he was shortly afterwards himself proclaimed emperor by these troops when they heard of the progress made in Italy by Æmilianus A.D. 253. He was kept on the throne by the assassination of Æmilianus. In a war with the Persians he was taken prisoner A.D. 260, and died in captivity A.D. 263, as it is generally believed, after having been treated very harshly. The well-preserved coin giving the features on Plate XCVIII. represents Valerian without a beard: this coin is in Mr. Blackmore's possession. A numismatic friend who saw the plate found fault with it, as he said it had been drawn from a worn specimen ; but, on the contrary, the coin is in a beautiful state of preservation. As, however, Valerian is more usually represented with a beard, a second Plate XCVIII. No. 2, is here given from another coin also in Mr. Blackmore's collection.

For the following remarks I am indebted to my numismatic friend mentioned above, and the reader will doubtless consider me right in transcribing them entire :—
' It is possible, however, that Plate XCVIII. is intended for Valerianus, junr., brother and colleague of Gallienus. But the history of that family is a complete enigma. Trebellius Pollio, only forty years later, is forced to confess : "Frater ejus Valerianus est interemptus, quem multi Augustum, multi Cæsarem, multi *neutrum* fuisse dicunt : quod verisimile non est, siquidem capto jam Valeriano scriptum invenimus in Fastis : ' Valeriano Imperatore Consule,' quis igitur alius potuit esse Valerianus nisi Gallieni frater ? Constat de genere, non satis tamen constat de dignitate, vel, ut cœperunt alii loqui, de *Majestate*." ' (Gallieni Duo xiv.)'

That this Valerian was emperor also appears from the expression of Gallienus, in his letter to Venerianus (Treb. Poll. Ingenuus), where he calls himself ' Tot principum pater et *frater*.'

PLATE XCIX.

MARINIANA.

1 B.—DIVAE MARINIANAE.

Mariniana is said to have been the wife of Valerianus, but she is only known by her coins. She certainly belonged to the family of Valerianus, but she may have been either his mother, or his sister, or his daughter.

The profile is taken from a sulphur cast of a 1 B. in the collection of Mr. Blackmore.

PLATE C.

GALLIENUS.

2 B.—IMP. GALLIENVS P.F. AVG.

Publius Licinius Gallienus, the son of Valerianus by his first wife, whose name is unknown, was born A.D. 218. He was associated in the empire by his father with the titles of Cæsar and Augustus A.D. 253. He reigned alone from the year A.D. 260, when Valerian was taken prisoner by the Persians. He was assassinated by conspirators at the siege of Milan, where the pretender Aureolus had taken refuge, A.D. 268.

PLATE CI.

SALONINA.

ARG.—SALONINA AVG.

Cornelia Salonina was married to Gallienus about ten years before he came to the throne. She was probably assassinated with her husband before Milan A.D. 268.

PLATE CII.

SALONINUS.

1 B.—P.C.S. VALERIANVS CAES.

Publius Licinius Cornelius Saloninus Valerianus Gallienus, the son of Gallienus and Salonina, was born A.D. 242.

He was made Cæsar by Valerianus at the time when Gallienus was associated in the empire A.D. 253. He was put to death in Gaul by Postumus, governor of that country, who had persuaded his legions to proclaim him emperor, A.D. 259.

The profile is taken from the sulphur cast of a 1 B. in Mr. Blackmore's collection.

PLATE CIII.

POSTUMUS.

3 B. Plated.—IMP. C. POSTVMUS P.F. AVG.

Marcus Cassianus Latinius Postumus was born, in Gaul, of obscure parentage. He was governor of that province under Valerianus, when he was proclaimed emperor by his legions A.D. 258. He was killed by his own soldiers A.D. 267, after the taking of the city of Mayence, where the usurper Lælianus had taken refuge.

PLATE CIV.

LÆLIANUS.

ARG.—IMP. C. LAELIANVS P.F. AVG.

Ulpius Cornelius Lælianus usurped the crown in Gaul under Postumus, who was killed, so that Lælianus remained for some months master of a part of that country, but was at length killed by his own soldiers at the instigation of Victorinus. These coins of Lælianus are said to be genuine ; but there are other coins which bear the names of Lollianus and Ælianus, which may, at least, be considered doubtful, and probably may be referred to Lælianus.

The coin from which the profile was drawn is in the collection of Mr. Blackmore.

PLATE CV.

VICTORINUS.

3 B.—IMP. C. VICTORINVS P.F. AVG.

Marcus Piauvonius Victorinus was a general in the army
of Postumus, and was associated by him in the empire
A.D. 265, as it is generally believed. He was assassinated
at Cologne shortly after the death of Postumus and
Lælianus.

PLATE CVI.

MARIUS.

ARG.—IMP. C. MARIVS P.F. AVG.

Marcus Aurelius Marius was born of low origin. He
was proclaimed emperor by the legions of Gaul after the
death of Victorinus A.D. 267. He was assassinated by a
soldier, after having reigned, it is said, only three days.

PLATE CVII.

TETRICUS (Senr.).

3 B.—IMP. C. TETRICVS P.F. AVG.

Caius Pesuvius Tetricus was born of senatorial ancestors.
He was governor of Aquitania under Valerianus and
Gallienus. He was chosen emperor by the army of Gaul,
A.D. 267, after the death of Marius, and a little before
that of Gallienus. After having maintained his authority
during the whole reign of Claudius Gothicus and a part
of the following reign, he voluntarily laid down the
imperial purple, and restored to Aurelianus the provinces
he had usurped, A.D. 272 or 273. He died in a private
station.

PLATE CVIII.

TETRICUS (Junr.).

3 B.—C. PIVESV. TETRICVS CAES.

Caius Pesuvius Pivesus Tetricus, the son of Tetricus, senr., was made Cæsar by his father A.D. 267. He retired into private life, on the abdication of his father, A.D. 272 or 273.

PLATE CIX.

MACRIANUS (Junr.).

Billon.—A.K.M. ΦOY. MAKPIANOC ЄY. ЄYC.

Marcus or Titus Fulvius Macrianus, to whom this coin may probably be referred, was the son of the elder Macrianus, none of whose coins are known. The father was general under Valerianus in his war against Persia ; and after this prince was made prisoner, A.D. 260, Macrianus, senr., was proclaimed emperor A.D. 260, and his son was made Augustus at the same time. Both were killed in Illyria, after having suffered a defeat by Aureolus.

This profile was taken from a cast of a coin in the British Museum. *See* 'Madden's Handbook of Roman Coins,' Plate II., fig. I., and some notice of the latter part of the legend, page 164 of the same volume.

PLATE CX.

QUIETUS.

3 B. Plated.—IMP. C. FVL. QVIETVS P.F. AVG.

Caius Fulvius Quietus was the son of the elder Macrianus, and was made Augustus at the same time as his father and his brother A.D. 260. Both of these princes having fallen in Illyria, Quietus was shut up in Emesa, and put to death when the town was taken by Odenathus, Prince of Palmyra, A.D. 262.

The coin from which this profile was taken is in Mr. Blackmore's collection.

PLATE CXI.

CLAUDIUS GOTHICUS.

3 B.—IMP. C. CLAVDIVS AVG.

Marcus Aurelius Claudius was born of an obscure family in Illyria A.D. 214 or 215. He was governor of that province under Valerianus and Gallienus. He was called into Italy A.D. 268 to secure Turin, while Gallienus led his troops against the usurper Aureolus, and after the death of Gallienus he was proclaimed Cæsar and Augustus by the army and the senate. He obtained a decided victory over the Goths in Upper Mœsia A.D. 269, and afterwards took the surname of Gothicus. He died of the plague, near Sirmium, in Pannonia, A.D. 270.

PLATE CXII.

QUINTILLUS.

3 B.—IMP. C.M. AVR. CL. QVINTILLVS AVG.

Marcus Aurelius Claudius Quintillus was the brother of Claudius Gothicus, and was proclaimed emperor by the army under his command, near Aquileia, on the death of his brother A.D. 270. But finding that he was abandoned by his soldiers on the news of the election of Aurelianus by the army of Pannonia, he killed himself by opening his veins, having reigned less than twenty days.

PLATE CXIII.

AURELIANUS.

3 B —IMP. AVRELIANVS AVG.

Lucius or Claudius Domitius Aurelianus was born at Sirmium, in Pannonia, of obscure parents, about A.D. 207.

He was general of the horse under Claudius Gothicus, and after the death of this prince he was proclaimed emperor by his troops A.D. 270. He was assassinated in Thrace A.D. 275, when about to march against the Persians.

The coin from which this profile was taken is in Mr. Blackmore's collection.

PLATE CXIV.

SEVERINA.

3 B.—SEVERINA AVG.

Ulpia Severina is hardly known, except as the wife of Aurelianus, and by her coins.

PLATE CXV.

ZENOBIA.

' Potin.'—CEΠTIMIA ZHNOBIA.

Zenobia was the wife of Odenathus, the king of Palmyra, who for his services against the Persians was associated in the empire and made Augustus by Gallienus A.D. 264. After his death Zenobia took the titles of Augusta and Queen of the East, and governed in the name of her son to A.D. 273, when she was defeated and made prisoner by Aurelianus. She ended her days on an estate near Rome, which had been given to her by her conqueror.

The coin from which this sketch was taken is in the British Museum.

PLATE CXVI.

VABALATHUS.

3 B.—VABALATHVS VCRIMDR.

Vabalathus Athenodorus was the son of Zenobia. On his coins he is called Vabalathus VCRIMDR, the meaning of which is problematical. He was associated in the empire in Syria and Egypt, together with his brothers, by Zenobia

A.D. 266 or 267. He was taken prisoner with her by Aurelianus A.D. 273.   After this his history is unknown.

The coin from which this profile was drawn is in Mr. Blackmore's collection.

PLATE CXVII.

TACITUS.

3 B.—IMP. C.M. CL. TACITVS AVG.

Marcus Claudius Tacitus was a senator and a man of consular dignity, a descendant of Tacitus the historian. He was chosen emperor by the senate A.D. 275 after an interregnum of six months from the death of Aurelianus. He died at Tarsus, in Cilicia, or at Tyane, in Cappadocia, by one account of illness, and according to others assassinated by his soldiers, A.D. 276. He only reigned six months.

PLATE CXVIII.

FLORIANUS.

B. Medallion.—IMP. C.M. ANN. FLORIANVS AVG.

Marcus Annius Florianus, the brother of Tacitus, was the Prætorian præfect during his short reign. After the death of Tacitus, he was proclaimed emperor by the army of Cilicia, and acknowledged by all the empire except Syria, which espoused the cause of Probus, A.D. 276. Florianus was killed by his own soldiers in about three months, as he was about to dispute the crown with Probus.

PLATE CXIX.

PROBUS.

3 B.—IMP. PROBVS P.F. AVG.

Marcus Aurelius Probus was born at Sirmium, in Pannonia, in the middle rank of life, A.D. 232. He was præfect of the East under the preceding emperors, and after the death of Tacitus he was proclaimed Augustus by the army of that district. On the death of Florianus he was acknowledged by the senate and the whole empire A.D. 276. He was murdered by his own soldiers in his native city as he was preparing for war with Persia A.D. 282.

PLATE CXX.

CARUS.

1 B.—IMP. C.M. AVR. CARVS P.F. AVG.

Marcus Aurelius Carus was born at Narbonne, in Gaul, about A.D. 230, of one of the old families of Rome. He was Prætorian præfect under Probus, and after his death was chosen emperor by the army of Pannonia, and was confirmed in his authority by the senate A.D. 282. He was killed the following year by lightning, near Ctesiphon, a city of Assyria, which he had just taken.

PLATE CXXI.

NUMERIANUS.

3 B. Plated.—IMP. NVMERIANVS P.F. AVG.

Marcus Aurelius Numerianus was the younger son of Carus, and was born A.D. 254. He was made Cæsar by his father A.D. 282, and accompanied him the following year on his expedition against Persia. He was there made emperor, but had not then the title of Augustus. On his father's death A.D. 283 he was made emperor and Augustus by the army of the East jointly with Carinus, his elder brother, who remained in the West. He was assassinated A.D. 284 by Arrius Aper, his father-in-law, the Prætorian præfect.

PLATE CXXII.

CARINUS.

B. Medallion.—IMP. C.M. AVR. CARINVS P.F. AVG.

Marcus Aurelius Carinus, the elder son of Carus, was born A.D. 249. He was made Cæsar by his father A.D. 282 at the same time as his brother Numerianus. He remained in the West while his father and brother were warring with Persia, and governed these provinces with the title of emperor, but without that of Augustus. On the death of his father he took this title A.D. 283 at the same time as Numerianus took it in the East. He was assassinated in Mœsia A.D. 285, soon after having gained a victory over Diocletianus, who had been chosen emperor by the army of the East after the death of Numerianus.

PLATE CXXIII.

MAGNIA URBICA.

B. Medallion.—MAGNIA VRBICA AVG.

Magnia Urbica is believed to have been the wife of Carinus, and is only known by her coins.

PLATE CXXIV.

NIGRINIANUS.

ARG.—DIVO NIGRINIANO.

Nigrinianus was probably the son of Carinus, but nothing is known of him except by his coins.

PLATE CXXV.

JULIANUS I.

3 B.—IVLIANVS P.F. AVG.

Marcus Aurelianus Julianus was the governor of the

province of Venetia under Carus and his sons.   After the death of Numerianus he usurped the title of emperor, and was acknowledged also by Pannonia, A.D. 284.   He was, however, defeated by Carinus, and killed near Verona the following year, having only worn the imperial purple five or six months.

The coin from which this profile was drawn is in the collection of Mr. Blackmore.

PLATE CXXVI.

DIOCLETIANUS.

2 B.—IMP. DIOCLETIANVS P.F. AVG.

Caius Valerius Diocletianus was born of obscure parentage at Dioclea, in Dalmatia, A.D. 245.   He was general of the legions of Mœsia under Probus.   He accompanied Carus on his expedition against Persia, and after his death A.D. 283 he attached himself to Numerianus.   When this prince was assassinated, Diocletianus was proclaimed Augustus by the army of the East A.D 284, and his position was secured by the death of Carinus the following year.   In the year 286, at Nicomedia, in Bithynia, he made Maximianus Herculeus his associate in the empire with the title of Augustus, and gave up to him the government of the West, reserving that of the Eastern provinces to himself. A.D. 292, in the same city, he adopted Galerius Maximianus, and made him Cæsar, at the time that Constantius Chlorus was adopted and made Cæsar by Maximianus Herculeus.   In the year A.D. 305 he abdicated the empire at Nicomedia, after naming Galerius Maximianus Augustus and Maximinus Daza Cæsar ; and in a similar way Maximianus Herculeus abdicated at Milan, after naming Constantius Chlorus Augustus and Severus Cæsar. Diocletianus retired to Salona, a city of Dalmatia, and died there A.D. 313.

PLATE CXXVII.

MAXIMIANUS HERCULEUS.

2 B.—IMP. C. MAXIMIANVS P.F. AVG.

Marcus Aurelius Valerius Maximianus (commonly called Maximianus Hercules or Herculeus) was born of low origin, near Sirmium, in Pannonia, A.D. 250. He was associated in the empire by Diocletianus A.D. 286, with the title of Augustus ; he had probably been made Cæsar the previous year. In the year A.D. 292 he adopted Constantius Chlorus, and gave him the title of Cæsar. A.D. 305 he abdicated at Milan, when Diocletianus did the same at Nicomedia ; and Constantius Chlorus was named Augustus and Severus Cæsar by Maximianus Herculeus ; while Galerius Maximianus was made Augustus and Maximinus Daza Cæsar by Diocletianus. The following year, however, Maximianus Herculeus resumed the title of emperor at Rome, at the solicitation of his son Maxentius, who took the title of Augustus. The father, having tried in vain to deprive his son of the purple, was obliged to leave Rome, and withdrew A.D. 308 into Gaul, after having abdicated a second time. He took up his quarters in the palace of his son-in-law Constantine, at Arles, and during the absence of Constantine corrupted the troops, and was proclaimed emperor a third time A.D. 309 ; but Constantine having returned, Maximianus was obliged to fly to Marseilles, where he was made prisoner and deprived of the purple ; still, however, he continued to reside in the palace of his son-in-law. At length, having again conspired against him, he was condemned to die, and, the choice of his death being left to him, he strangled himself A.D. 310.

PLATE CXXVIII.

CARAUSIUS.

AUR.—CARAVSIVS P.F. AVG.

Marcus Aurelius Valerius Carausius was born, in Belgian

Gaul, of obscure parentage. He was entrusted by Maximianus Herculeus with the command of a fleet intended to defend the coasts of Great Britain and Belgian Gaul, and went with this fleet to Britain, where he was proclaimed emperor A.D. 287. He retained his position so far against the forces sent against him that Maximianus was obliged by treaty to give to Carausius the title of Augustus, and to leave him master of Great Britain, A.D. 289. Carausius was assassinated by Allectus, one of his officers, A.D. 293.

PLATE CXXIX.

ALLECTUS.

AUR.—IMP. C. ALLECTVS P.F. AVG.

Allectus (a usurper in Britain under Diocletianus) was the lieutenant of Carausius, after whose assassination he was proclaimed emperor A.D. 293, but was killed in battle A.D. 296 by Asclepiodorus, a general of Constantius Chlorus.

PLATE CXXX.

CONSTANTIUS CHLORUS.

1 B.—FL. VAL. CONSTANTIVS NOB. C.

Flavius Valerius Constantius, the son of Eutropius and Claudia, the daughter of Crispus, the brother of Claudius Gothicus (commonly called Chlorus), was born in Upper Mœsia about A.D. 250. He was made governor of Dalmatia by Carus A.D. 282. He was adopted and made Cæsar by Maximianus Herculeus at the time when Galerius Maximianus was adopted and made Cæsar by Diocletianus. He obtained for his share of the empire Gaul, Spain, and Great Britain. He was proclaimed Augustus at Milan by Maximianus Herculeus, who abdicated, in the same way as Galerius Maximianus was proclaimed Augustus at Nicomedia by Diocletianus, who also abdicated A.D. 305. He died at York the following year, after having made his son Constantine Cæsar.

PLATES CXXXI. AND CXXXIa.

HELENA.

PLATE CXXXI.

B. Medallion.—FL. HELENA AVGVSTA.

PLATE CXXXIa.

3 B.—FL. HELENA AVGVSTA.

Flavia Julia Helena, the first wife of Constantius Chlorus, was born of an obscure family at Drepanum, in Bithynia, A.D. 248. She had been married to Constantius Chlorus some time before he became Cæsar; but she was then divorced, as Constantius was obliged to marry Theodora, the daughter-in-law of Maximianus Herculeus. Subsequently she was honoured with the title of Augusta by her son Constantine. It is believed that she died at Rome A.D. 328.

This profile of Plate CXXXI. is taken from the cast of a bronze medallion in the British Museum; but though this is doubtless the best likeness of Helena extant, yet the coin is so rare that it has been deemed advisable to give a second plate, Plate CXXXIA., from the 3 B. far more generally known: it is from Mr. Blackmore's collection. Some writers consider the coins of Helena, whose name is followed by the letters N.F., to belong to this princess; but the reader is referred to the extract from the Rev. C. W. King's 'Christian Numismatics,' given under Helena, the wife of Julianus II., which appears to prove very clearly that Helena N.F. cannot be the Helena the mother of Constantine. The extract which is given nearly entire will fully explain Mr. King's views, and his arguments certainly appear to have much weight.

PLATE CXXXIB.

THEODORA.

3 B.—FL. MAX. THEODORAE AVG.

Flavia Maximiana Theodora was the daughter of Eutropia, the daughter-in-law of Maximianus Herculeus, was the second wife of Constantius Chlorus, and was married to him when he became Cæsar A.D. 292.

PLATE CXXXII.

GALERIUS MAXIMIANUS.

3 B.—GAL. VAL. MAXIMIANVS NOB. CAES.

Galerius Valerius Maximianus, the son-in-law of Diocletianus, was born, near Sardica, of low origin. He was adopted and made Cæsar by Diocletianus A.D. 292, and obtained for his share of the empire the administration of Thrace and Illyria. He was proclaimed Augustus at Nicomedia by Diocletianus, who resigned the purple A.D. 305. Galerius died A.D. 311.

PLATE CXXXIII.

VALERIA.

AUR.—GAL. VALERIA AVG.

Galeria Valeria, the daughter of Diocletianus, was the second wife of Galerius Maximianus, and was married to him when made Cæsar A.D. 292. She was put to death by the orders of Licinius A.D. 315.

PLATE CXXXIV.

FLAVIUS SEVERUS.

ARG.—SEVERVS AVGVST.

Flavius Valerius Severus was born in Illyria of unknown parentage. He was made Cæsar by Maximianus Herculeus on the abdication of that emperor in the place of Constantius Chlorus, who was made Augustus A.D. 305. After the death of Constantius Chlorus A.D. 306, Flavius Severus was proclaimed Augustus and emperor by Galerius

Maximianus A.D. 306. He was sent by Galerius against Maxentius, the son of Maximianus Herculeus, who had assumed the purple at Rome ; but he was besieged in Ravenna by Maximianus, who made him prisoner and put him to death A.D. 313.

PLATE CXXXV.

MAXIMINUS DAZA.

2 B.—GAL. VAL. MAXIMINVS NOB. C.

Galerius Valerius Maximinus, the son of the sister of Galerius Maximianus (commonly called Maximinus Daza), was born of low parentage in Illyria. He was made Cæsar by Diocletianus when he abdicated the throne in the place of Galerius Maximianus who became Augustus A.D. 305. Galerius having made Licinius Augustus in the place of Severus, who had been put to death by Maximianus Herculeus, Maximinus received at the same time as Constantine the title of 'Filius Augustorum' A.D. 307. Not content with this title, the following year he assumed the title of emperor, and was proclaimed by the army of the East, which was under his orders, and he was soon acknowledged as such by his uncle. Having made war with Licinius, he was defeated in Thrace, and fled to Tarsus, in Cilicia, where he took poison and died miserably A.D. 313.

PLATE CXXXVI.

MAXENTIUS.

2 B.—MAXENTIVS P.F. AVG.

Marcus Aurelius Valerius Maxentius, the son of Maximianus Herculeus and Eutropia, and the son-in-law of Galerius Maximianus, was born about A.D. 282. As he considered himself neglected when Severus and Maximinus Daza were promoted, and also when Constantine was made Cæsar, he assumed the title of emperorat Rome, and was proclaimed as such by the senate and the Prætorian guards: he also persuaded his father to reassume the purple A.D. 306. He maintained his position against Flavius Severus and Galerius Maximianus who attacked him successively, and he then invaded Africa, and was recognised there as emperor A.D. 308. Having declared war against Constantine he was defeated in a battle with him near Rome, and in his flight was drowned in the Tiber, A.D. 312.

PLATE CXXXVII.

ROMULUS CÆSAR.

2 B.—DIVO ROMVLO NVBIS CONS.

Marcus Aurelius Romulus, the son of Maxentius, was born, it is thought, A.D. 306. He was made Cæsar by his father the following year, and Augustus some time after. He died A.D. 309.

With respect to the words or letters Nvbis Cons., Mionnet says that the meaning is entirely unknown; but Mr. F. W. Madden, in his 'Handbook,' page 136, adopts the reading of a French numismatist thus: *Nobilissimo Viro* BIS CON*Suli.*

PLATE CXXXVIII.

LICINIUS (Senr.).

3 B.—IMP. LICINIVS P.F. AVG.

Publius Flavius Claudius Galerius Valerius Licinianus Licinius, who married the sister of Constantinus Maximus, and who consequently was the son-in-law of Constantius Chlorus, was born of an obscure family, in Dacia, about A.D. 263. He was made Cæsar and Augustus and associated in the empire by Galerius Maximianus after the death of Severus A.D. 307. He allied himself with Constantine, and married his sister Constantia A.D. 313. He then quarrelled with him and declared war the following year, but he was defeated in several battles and was obliged to sue for peace. It was agreed that he should retain the East, while Constantine governed the West. War again broke out between him and his brother-in-law A.D. 323; but he lost two pitched battles, one at Hadrianopolis and the other at Chrysopolis, near Chalcedon, and was obliged to give himself up to the conqueror, who banished him to Thessalonica, and had him strangled the same year.

PLATE CXXXIX.

LICINIUS (JUNR.).

3 B.—D.N. VAL. LICIN. LICINIVS NOB. C.

Flavius Valerius Licinianus Licinius, the son of Licinius, senr., and Constantia, was born A.D. 315. He was made Cæsar A.D. 317. After the death of his father this title was taken away from him A.D. 323. He was put to death by the orders of Constantine A.D. 326.

From Mr. Blackmore's collection.

PLATES CXL. CXLa. AND CXLb.

CONSTANTINUS MAXIMUS.

PLATE CXL.

AUR. MEDALLION.—(NO LEGEND).

PLATE CXLa.

2 B.—IMP. CONSTANTINVS P.F. AVG.

PLATE CXLb.

AUR.—D.N. CONSTANTINVS MAX. AVG.

Flavius Galerius Valerius Constantinus, the son of Constantius Chlorus and Helena, son-in-law of Maximianus Herculeus, and brother to the wife of Licinius, was born at

Naissus, in Dardania, A.D. 274. Immediately on the death of his father he was proclaimed Cæsar and Augustus by the army of Constantius Chlorus A.D. 306 ; but as Galerius Maximianus refused him the title of Augustus, he remained content with that of Cæsar. But the following year he was again honoured with the title of Augustus by Maximianus Herculeus, who gave him his daughter Fausta in marriage ; but Constantine still was satisfied with the title of 'Filius Augustorum,' which was also given to Maximinus Daza A.D. 308. Maximinus having taken the title of Augustus with the consent of the army of the East, Constantine at last received it from Galerius, and was recognised as Augustus by the whole empire. He was converted to Christianity A.D. 311. After the death of Galerius Maximianus, which happened the same year, he successively got rid of his other colleagues, Maxentius, Maximinus Daza, and Licinius, and reigned alone after A.D. 323. He transferred the seat of empire from Rome to Byzantium, in Thrace, and altered the name of that city to Constantinopolis, A.D. 330. He died near Nicomedia, in Bithynia, when about to make war with Persia, A.D. 337.

The handsome and well-executed coin from which the profile, Plate CXL., was taken, is in the British Museum. A woodcut of it is given in page 3 of the Rev. C. W. King's ' Early Christian Numismatics.' The reader will find much curious information in this volume respecting Constantinus, and at pages xvii. and 55 especial reference to this gold coin. The more usual profile of Constantinus is given on Plate CXLA., which is 2 B. and in every collection. Plate CXLB., from a gold medallion in the British Museum, represents Constantine in his imperial robes : the coin is remarkably handsome. It may, however, be right to append the remarks of a friend well versed in numismatics respecting this latter plate. He says : ' It may possibly be the portrait of Constantinus junr. ; the features certainly are more youthful than those in the two preceding plates. Coins to a large amount must necessarily have been struck by the son during the three years that he enjoyed the dignity of Augustus ; but they can only be discriminated by the uncertain criterion of the portraits, for the young emperor had audaciously appropriated his predecessor's title of " Maximus." [1]

PLATE CXLI.

FAUSTA.

3 B.—FLAV. MAX. FAVSTA AVG.

Flavia Maxima Fausta, the daughter of Maximianus Herculeus and Eutropia, and the sister of Maxentius, was born at Rome, and was married to Constantine A.D. 307, but was suffocated in a warm bath by his orders A.D. 326, for having falsely accused Crispus.

PLATE CXLII.

CRISPUS.

ARG.—CRISPVS NOB. CAES.

Flavius Julius Crispus, the son of Constantinus Maximus and Minervina, and step-son to Fausta, was born in the East about A.D. 300. He was made Cæsar by his father and Licinius, at the same time as Licinius, junr., and Constantinus, junr., A.D. 317. He was put to death by order of his father on a false accusation brought against him by his step-mother Fausta.

PLATE CXLIII.

DELMATIUS.

3 B.—FL. DELMATIVS NOB. CAES.

Flavius Julius Delmatius, the son of Delmatius the brother of Constantine and the grandson of Constantius Chlorus, was born at Toulouse, or, according to other ac-

counts, at Narbonne.   He was made Cæsar by his uncle
A.D. 335, and received for his share the administration of
Thrace, Macedonia, and Achaia.   He was put to death by
the soldiery after the decease of his uncle, as they would
recognisè no one as emperor who was not the son of Constantine.

PLATE CXLIV.

HANNIBALIANUS.

3 B.—FL. CL. HANNIBALIANO REGI.

Flavius Claudius Hannibalianus, the brother of Delmatius, was born at Toulouse.   He had the title of king given
to him by his uncle, together with the provinces of Pontus,
Cappadocia, and Armenia, A.D. 335.   He was assassinated,
like his brother, by the soldiery, after the death of Constantine, A.D. 337.

The profile is drawn from the cast of a coin in the
British Museum.

PLATE CXLV.

CONSTANTINUS II. (or Junr.).

3 B.—CONSTANTINVS IVN. NOB. C.

Flavius Claudius Julius Constantinus, the eldest son
of Constantinus Maximus and Fausta, was born at Arles
A.D. 316.   He was made Cæsar the following year by his
father and Licinius at the same time as Crispus and Licinius,
junr.   In the division of the empire made by his father, A.D.
335, he obtained for his share Gaul, Spain, and Great Britain.
After the death of his father, A.D. 337, he was acknowledged
Augustus, as well as his brothers Constantius and Constans,
both by the senate and the army.   He was defeated and
killed near Aquileia, in Italy, by the troops of Constans,
whose territory he had invaded, A.D. 340.

PLATE CXLVI.

CONSTANS.

1 B.—D.N. FL. CONSTANS AVG.

Flavius Julius Constans, the youngest son of Constantinus Maximus and Fausta, was born about A.D. 320. He was made Cæsar by his father A.D. 333, and A.D. 335 obtained for his share of the empire Italy, Illyria, and Africa. On the death of Constantine, A.D. 337, he, as well as his brothers, was acknowledged as emperor. After the death of Constantinus, junr., who was killed under the walls of Aquileia, he remained master of all the West. He was assassinated in the Pyrenees by emissaries of the usurper Magnentius, who had assumed the imperial purple in Gaul, A.D. 350.

PLATES CXLVII. CXLVIIA. AND CXLVIIB.

CONSTANTIUS II. (or JUNR.).

PLATE CXLVII.

3 B.—FL. IVL. CONSTANTIVS NOB. C.

PLATE CXLVIIA.

AUR.—FL. IVL. CONSTANTIVS PERP. AVG.

PLATE CXLVIIB.

AUR.—D.N. CONSTANTIVS MAX. AVG.

Flavius Julius Constantius, the son of Constantinus Maximus and Fausta, was born at Sirmium, in Pannonia, A.D. 317. He was made Cæsar by his father A.D. 323, and received the East for his share of the empire. He was made Augustus at the same time as his brothers A.D. 337. He became sole master of the empire after the death of Constans A.D. 350. He died at Mopsucrene, in Cilicia, A.D. 351, as he was preparing for war with Julianus, his cousin, who had been made Cæsar by him, but who had assumed the title of Augustus in Gaul.

Plate CXLVII. represents him as Cæsar, Plates CXLVII. A. and B. give his features as emperor.   The latter gives his full face.   Both these are drawn from casts of coins in the British Museum.

PLATE CXLVIIc.

FAUSTA.

3 B.—FAVSTA N.F.   (Rev. Sunstar [blazing sun] in wreath).

Fausta is believed by many authors to have been the wife of Constantius II., whose first wife is mentioned in history but without giving her name, though she appears to have been the daughter of Julius Constantius, the brother of Constantinus Maximus : Julian, in his Epistle to the Athenians (as a friend has reminded me), says that Constantius II. had married a sister of Gallus, the son of Julius Constantius.   The Fausta now represented cannot have been the wife of Constantinus Maximus from the title N.F. (or, Nobilissima Fœmina).—See the remarks of Mr. King, copied under Helena N.F. (Juliani), but it is quite in accordance with Roman usage that her *niece* should have been married after her.

The profile is taken from the cast of a coin in the British Museum.

PLATE CXLVIII.

NEPOTIANUS.

AUR.—FL. POP. NEPOTIANVS P.F. AVG.

Flavius Popilius Nepotianus Constantinus, the son of Eutropia, the sister of Constantinus Maximus, assumed the imperial purple at Rome after the death of his cousin Constans A.D. 350, but was killed about twenty-eight days afterwards in a battle with Marcellinus, the prime minister of Magnentius.

The profile is taken from the cast of a coin in the British Museum.

PLATE CXLIX.

VETRANIO.

AUR.—D.N. VETRANIO P.F. AVG.

Vetranio was born in Upper Mœsia. When general of infantry under Constantius, junr., he was proclaimed emperor at Sirmium, in Pannonia, after the death of Constans, A.D. 350. He was, however, in the same year obliged by Constantius to lay aside the purple, after a short reign of less than ten months, and retired to Prusa, in Bithynia, where he ended his life about A.D. 356.

From the cast of a coin in the British Museum.

PLATE CL.

MAGNENTIUS.

2 B.—D.N. MAGNENTIVS P.F. AVG.

Flavius Magnus Magnentius was born of foreign parentage, either in Great Britain or in Germany, about A.D. 303. When commanding the guards of the Emperor Constans he assumed the title of emperor at Augustodunum, in Lyonese Gaul, and was the means of Constans being assassinated, A.D. 350. After having been twice defeated by Constantius he killed himself A.D. 353.

PLATE CLI.

DECENTIUS.

B. MEDALLION.—MAG. DECENTIVS NOB. CAES.

Magnus Decentius, the brother of Magnentius, was made Cæsar by him at Milan A.D. 351, but killed himself on hearing of his brother's tragic fate.

PLATE CLII.

CONSTANTIUS GALLUS.

1 B.—D.N. FL. CL. CONSTANTIVS NOB. CAES.

Flavius Claudius Julius Constantius Gallus, the son of Julius Constantius (the brother of Constantinus Maximus) and Galla, was the cousin of Constantius, junr., and married his sister. He was born A.D. 325, and was made Cæsar by the Emperor Constantius, junr., who gave him his sister Constantina to wife, A.D. 351. He was put to death by order of his brother-in-law A.D. 354, after having shown that he was totally unfit for the purple.

PLATES CLIII., CLIV., CLV., AND CLVI.

JULIANUS II. (or the Apostate).

PLATE CLIII.—As CÆSAR.

ARG.—D.N. IVLIANVS NOB. CAES.

PLATE CLIV.—As EMPEROR.

AUR.—FL. CL. IVLIANVS P.F. AVG.

PLATE CLV.—(Ditto with HELENA his Wife, as SERAPIS and ISIS).

3 B.—DEO SARAPIDI (*sic*) Rev. VOTA PVBLICA.

PLATE CLVI. (Ditto).

3 B. –* * ARA * * Rev. VOTA PVBLICA.

Flavius Claudius Julianus, the son of Julius Constantius (the brother of Constantinus Maximus) and Basilina, was half-brother of Constantius Gallus, and cousin of Constantius, junr., and the husband of his sister. He was born at Constantinople A.D. 331. He was made Cæsar by the Emperor Constantius, junr., who gave him his sister Helena in marriage. He was proclaimed emperor against his own inclinations, by his army, at Paris, A.D. 360, and he retained his position on the throne by the death of Constantius, which happened in the following year. He was pierced with a javelin in a battle with the Persians on the banks of the Tigris, and expired soon afterwards, A.D. 363.

It is well known that Julianus in his early life was a Christian; but when he became, as emperor, more entirely his own master, he apostatised to heathenism. A number of coins were minted by him with various heathen symbols, and amongst these the most interesting are those which represent him and his wife Helena under the form of Serapis and Isis. The profiles of two of these coins are given in Plates CLV. and CLVI., and probably no one will doubt the appropriation. The modius on the head of Julianus, and the lotus, sacred to Isis, on that of Helena, are very remarkable. The two previous Plates, CLIII. and CLIV., represent him as Cæsar and as emperor.

The coins from which Plates CLIV., CLV., and CLVI. were drawn are in the British Museum.

PLATE CLVII.

HELENA.

3 B.—HELENA N.F. (Rev. Sunstar [blazing sun] in wreath).

Helena was the daughter of Constantinus Maximus and Fausta, and was married to Julianus when Cæsar A.D. 355. She died shortly after her husband had been proclaimed Augustus by the Gallic troops A.D. 360.

In the appropriation of this Helena N.F. to the wife of Julianus the opinion of Mr. King has been followed; and, as his arguments appear to be of very great weight, it seems correct to give them entire, and not be satisfied with a mere reference to the passage. The following extract, copied by his permission from his ‘Early Christian Numismatics’ (pp. 36–39), is in fact a summary of the case :—

‘ Garucci is certainly wrong in assigning the coins with reverse of the sunstar within a wreath to the mother and wife of Constantine. The Helena and Fausta whose coins exhibit this remarkable symbol both take in the legend the title of N.F. Now this title " Nobilissima Fœmina " is beyond all doubt the feminine equivalent to " Nobilissimus Cæsar," the regular style at that period of the next in succession to the empire ; consequently such a title would never have belonged to the Helena, Constantine's mother, whom her husband Constantius was forced to divorce in order to marry Theodora, Maximian's step-daughter—one chief condition of his elevation to the dignity of Cæsar. Helena, thus repudiated, remained in a private station until created *Augusta* by the filial piety of her son upon his own accession to the empire. She was at no time of her life the wife of a *Cæsar*, and consequently could not have borne the title appropriated strictly to that dignity. The case is yet stronger as regards Fausta, who was an *Augusta* from the first ; for her father Maximian, upon giving her in marriage to Constantine, raised him at the same time to the rank of an Augustus.

'The star type on both these coins will, however, enable us to ascertain indisputably who this Helena really was. This reverse is found on only three other coins : a second minimus with the bust and legend of " Populus Romanus," a denarius of Gallus, and another of his brother Julian, both proceeding from Gallic mints. There is, consequently, every probability that all coins bearing this very singular device were struck at the same time, and were inspired by the same motive. Now, Helena, youngest sister of Constantius II., wife of Julian, who governed Gaul with the rank of Cæsar only, would take of right the title of N.F. ; and the fact of this particular type being then actually in use at the Gallic mints, is an additional reason for assigning these very rare pieces to the *daughter*, not *mother*, of Constantine. She never enjoyed the dignity of Augusta, for she died during the celebration of the Quinquennalia by her husband at Paris, the first occasion on which he ventured to assume the pomp and jewelled diadem of an Augustus, having previously contented himself with a "simple wreath (*vili corona*) and purple robe, so that he looked like a trainer of athletes." (Ammian. xxi. 1.) As for the Fausta who uses the same style and type, it is now impossible to discover her identity; she may have been the wife of one of the cousins of Julian, whom, to their destruction, Constantine created Cæsars in the last year of his life. Some have supposed her the first wife of Constantius II. before his marriage to Eusebia, but this supposition rests upon no historical evidence; and these small copper coins are all of one and the same *fabrique*, and apparently issued about the date of Constantine's demise. But the most satisfactory explanation is the one quoted by Bauduri, which makes her a sister of Gallus and Julian, mentioned by the latter in his Epistle to the Athenians. Her portrait upon the rare coin preserving it is decidedly more juvenile than that of Fausta the empress; and the resemblance to the latter may be explained, either by the real family likeness of mother and daughter, or by the want of skill on the part of the engraver. On this supposition we have coins of Julian, his wife, brother, and sister, all issued at one and the same time (probably that of Julian's elevation to the rank of Cæsar), and stamped with the same auspicious device, the rarity of the medals of this younger Helena and Fausta being explained by the premature death of the two princesses.

'Lastly, the argument—a very strong one too—from *costume* comes in to settle the question. Helena *Augusta*, on her coins, wears the diadem due to her rank, and always has her back hair arranged in a large *queue*, carried upwards and fixed to the top of her head, after the fashion which prevailed in the century that gave her birth, and of which the latest example (beside her own) is exhibited by Valeria, daughter of Diocletian. But the Helena with the title N.F. wears her hair waved and tied up in a simple *chignon* at the back of her head, after the elegant antique fashion that had been revived by the better taste of the Fausta of whom there is every reason for supposing her the daughter. The old numismatists declared this Helena the wife of Crispus, from the fact of the two being named together in a law of that period; and Cohen shares all coins with the name of Helena equally between the mother and daughter of Constantine, not having perceived the stumbling-block to such attribution that lies in the difference of titles.'   He subsequently adds : 'Even if there be an *apparent* difference of portraits, the ownership of the coins of Helena, with the reverse *Securitas Reipublicæ*, is settled by the fact that they are found with the mint mark of *London*, which mint was given up *before* the dedication of Constantinople in 330, and therefore before the birth of Julian's Helena.'

To these remarks of Mr. King it may be well also to ask the reader's reference to the actual profiles of the two Helenas. If any one will compare Plates CXXXI. and CXXXIA. with Plates CLV., CLVI., and CLVII., he will at once see that the features of the profile drawn CXXXIA. are the same as those of the large medallion CXXXI.; while those of Helena N.F., Plate CLVII., are evidently intended for those of the faces drawn CLV. and CLVI., more especially the latter; and this agreement greatly strengthens Mr. King's theory.

In a letter lately received from the same friend, he urges that 'the strongest argument of all is derived from the *coiffure.* That first introduced by Julia Domna (in which the hair, made up in a long *queue*, was fastened to the top of the head) continued in fashion without the least variation for more than a century after her times. It was Fausta, Constantine's wife, who discarded it, and revived the infinitely more elegant style (waved and tied in a *chignon*) of her namesake, the wife of Marcus Aurelius. But the ladies of the previous generation, the widows of Constantius Chlorus, Helena and Theodora, adhered to the last to the fashion of their youth. And Fausta herself (in the medallion published by Cohen, and probably struck upon her marriage) still retains the Julia Domna *coiffure*, although all her subsequent coins exhibit her in that of her own invention. The Helena N.F. must consequently have flourished *after* the new fashion became the mode; and the comparison of portraits just adduced will satisfy every intelligent observer that she was the daughter of Fausta.'

PLATE CLVIII.

ROMULUS AUGUSTUS.

AUR.—D.N. ROMVLVS AVGVSTVS P.F. AVG.

After the time of Constantine and Julian it is in vain to look for portraits of the emperors on their coins: in fact, for years previously the portraiture on coins had been deteriorating, conventional features being used instead of the true ones. It may, however, be well, as a termination to the series, to give a sketch of the full face of Romulus Augustus (or Augustulus, as he is commonly called), not because it may be considered a likeness, but simply to show the state of the art at that time, and also because, though a mere phantom of royalty, he was actually the very last Emperor of the West. The sketch is from a cast of a gold coin.

Romulus Augustus was the son of Orestes, the master of the horse, and was proclaimed Augustus and Emperor of the West, A.D. 475, by Orestes, his father. But the following year he was deprived of the purple and sent into Campania by Odoacer, King of the Heruli, who was proclaimed King of Italy, thus putting an end to the Western Empire.

LONDON : PRINTED BY
SPOTTISWOODE AND CO., NEW-STREET SQUARE
AND PARLIAMENT STREET

F

POMPEIUS MAGNUS.

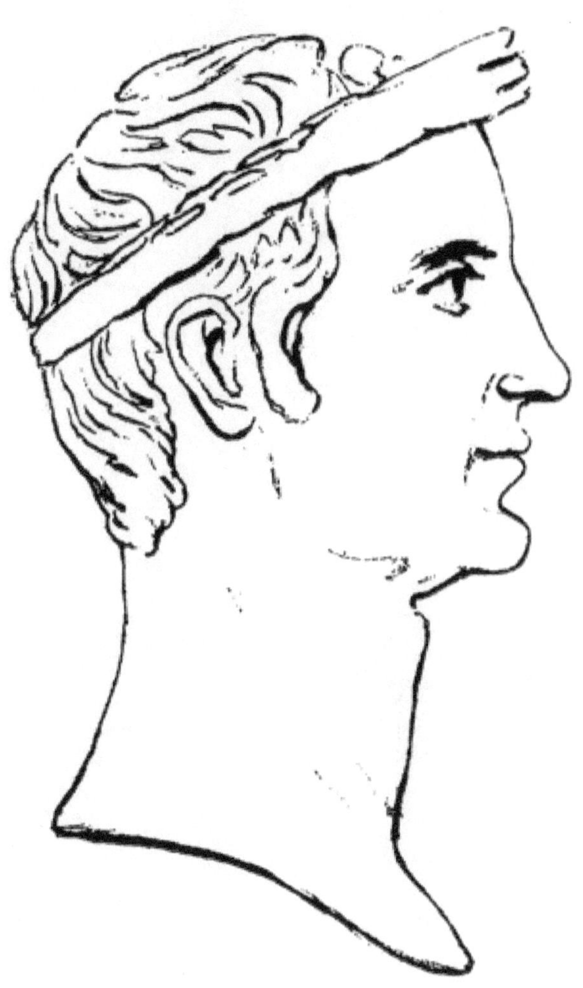

JULIUS.

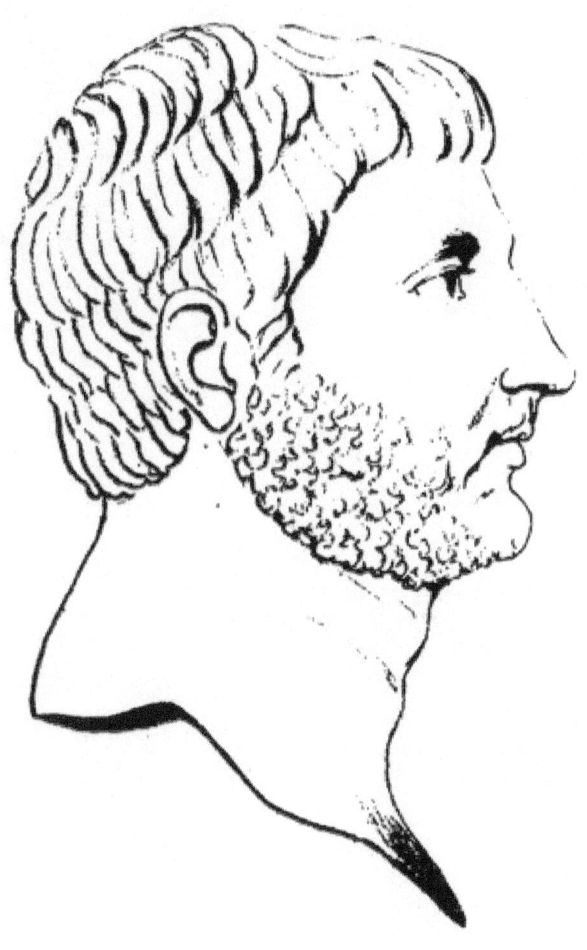

IV.

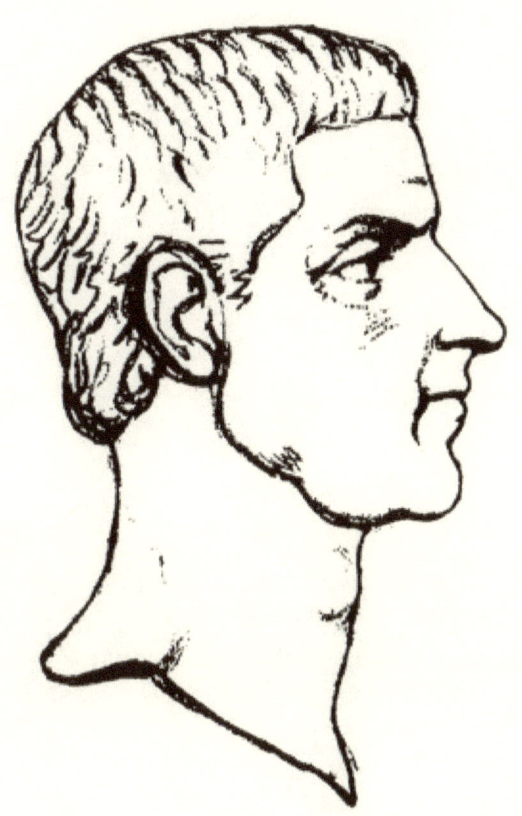

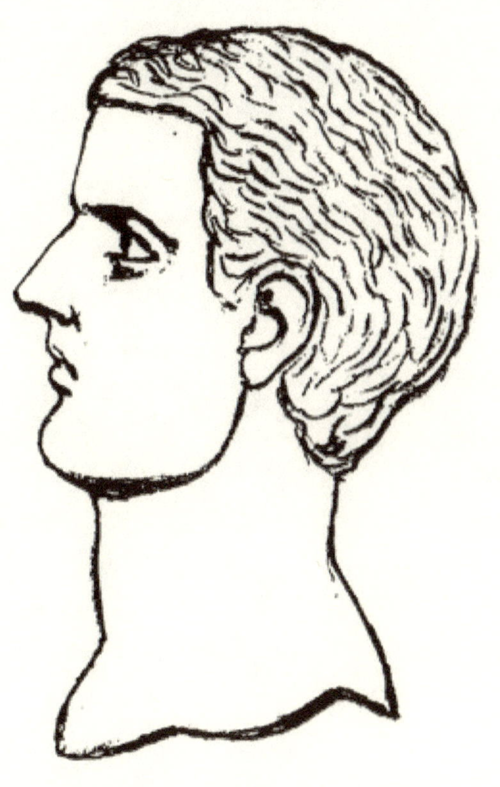

LEPIDUS.

MARCUS ANTONIUS.

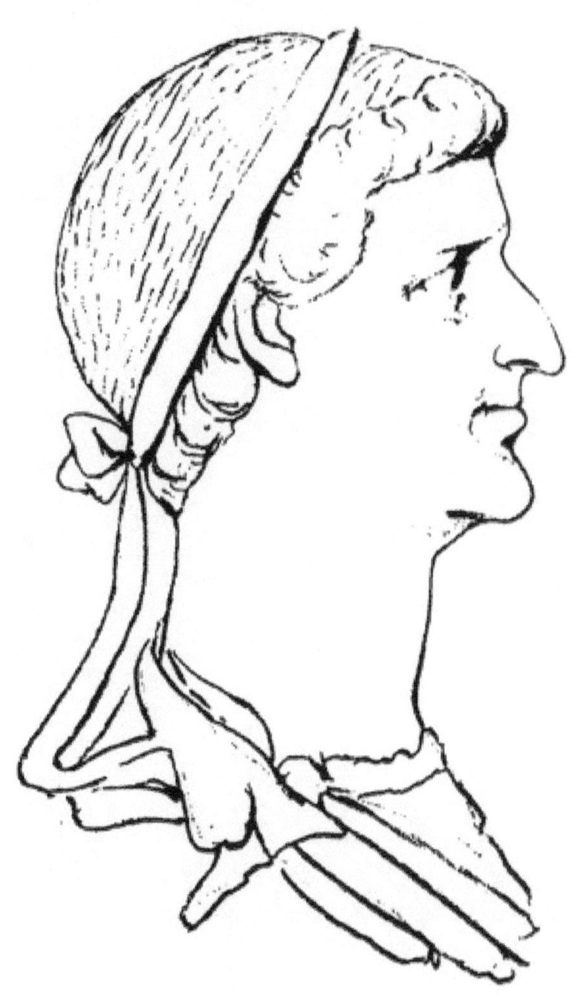

CLEOPATRA.

AUGUSTUS.

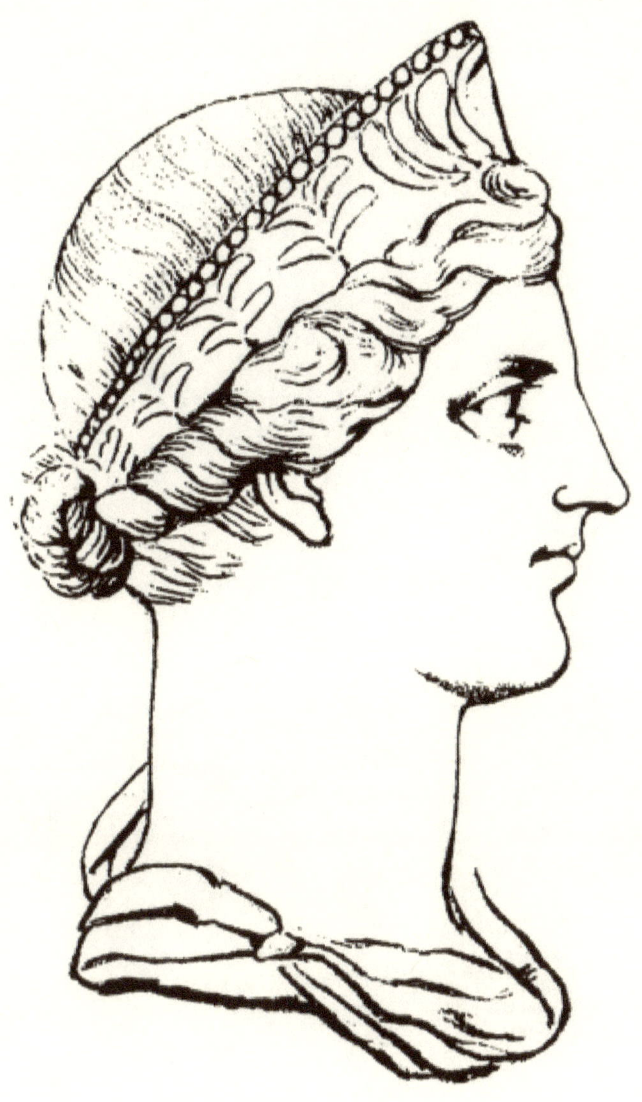

LIVIA, *(as Justitia.)*

LIVIA. *(as Pietas.)*

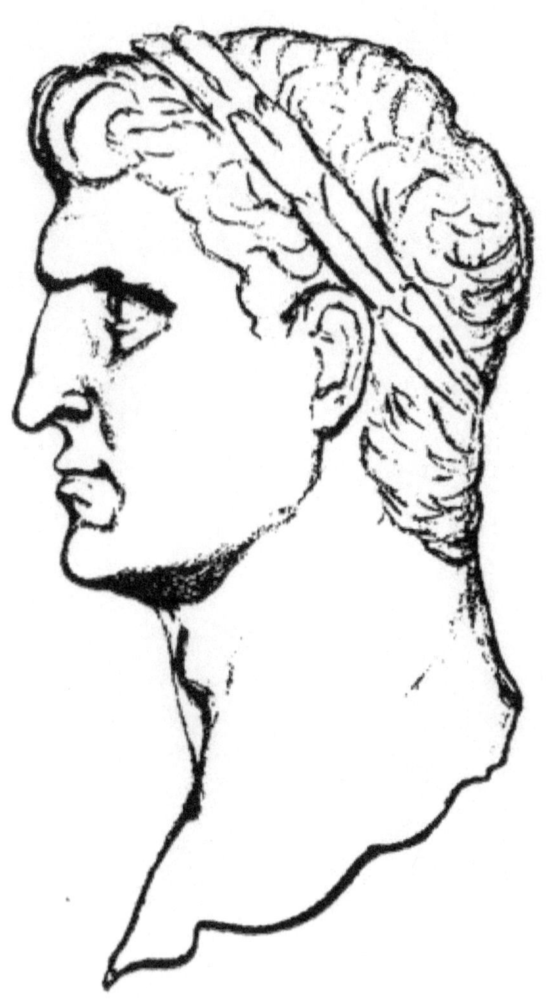

AGRIPPA.

AUGUSTI.

CAIUS CAESAR.

XV.

TIBERIUS.

JULIA AUGUSTI.

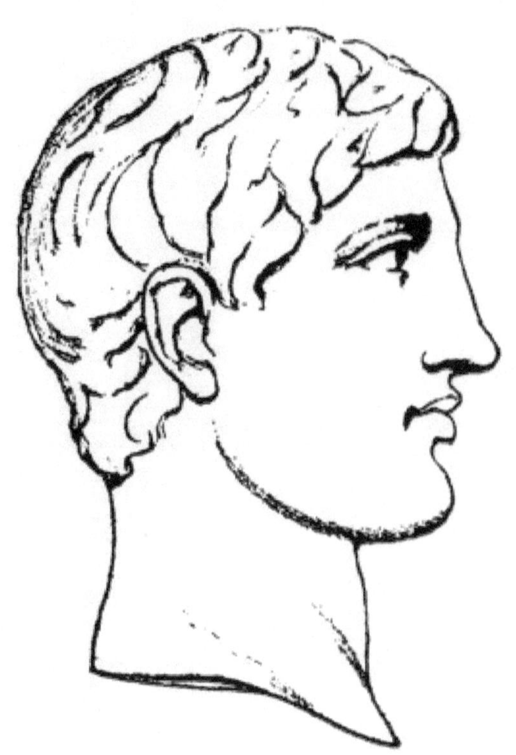

TIBERIUS.

DRUSUS *(Sen.ʳ)*

DRUSUS, *(Jun.ͬ)*

ANTONIA.

GERMANICUS.

AGRIPPINA
(Sen?)

XXII.

CLAUDIUS.

AGRIPPINA. (Jun.ʳ)

BRITANNICUS.

NERO.

POPPAEA.

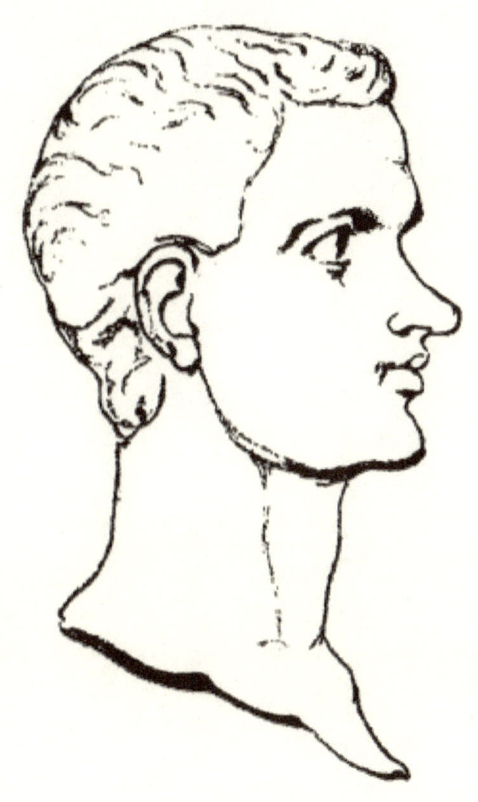

CLODIUS MACER.

GALBA.

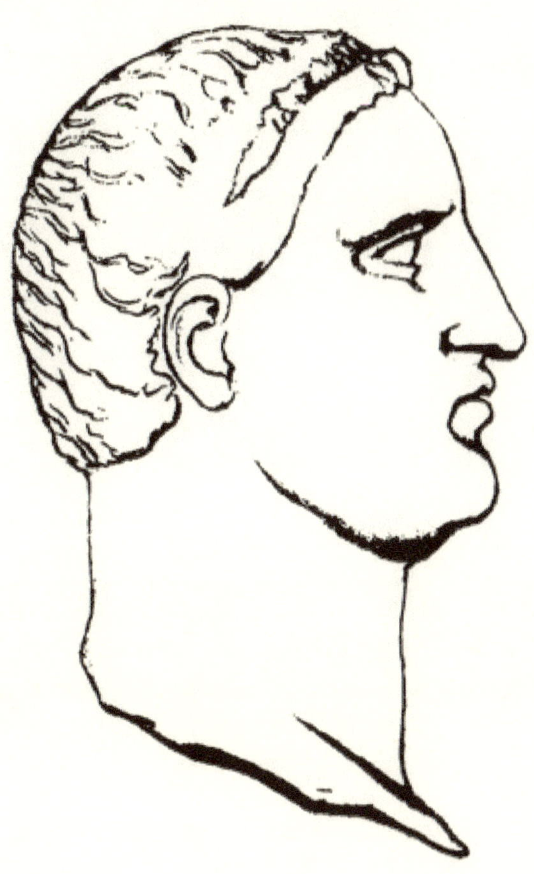

VITELLIUS.

VESPASIANUS.

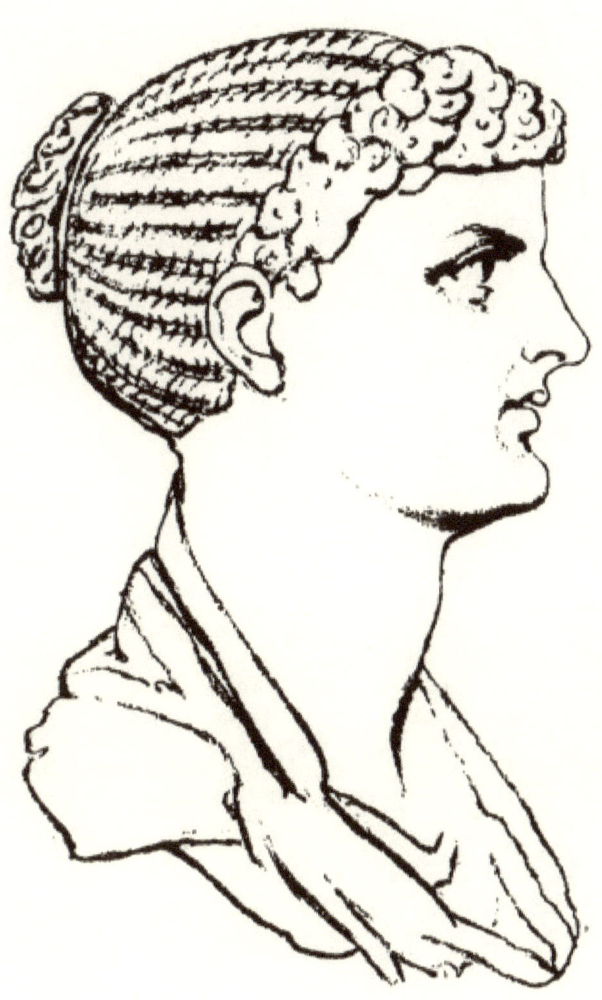

JULIA. *(Titi.)*

DOMITIANUS.

DOMITIA.

NERVA.

TRAJANUS.

PLOTINA.

MARCIANA.

MATIDIA.

HADRIANUS.

XLIII.
SABINA.

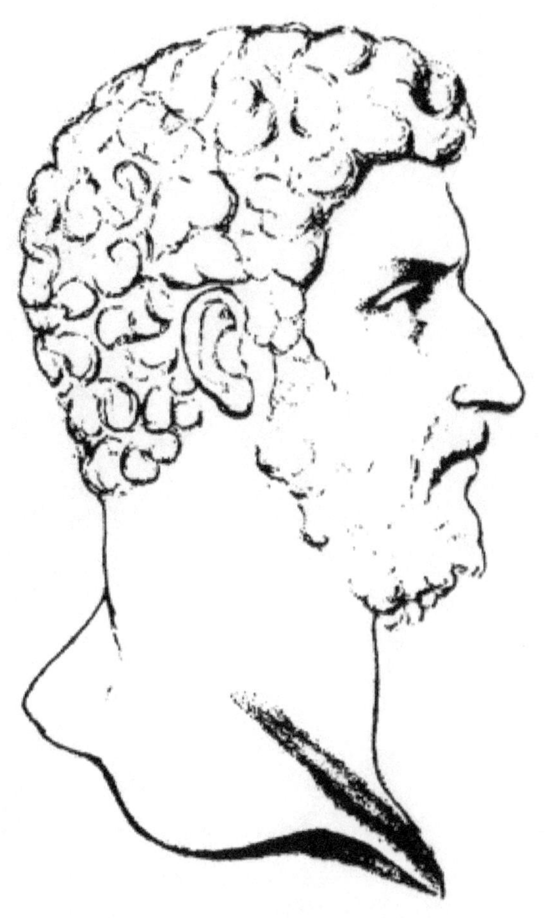

AELIUS CAESAR.

ANTONINUS PIUS.

FAUSTINA (Senᵣ.)

MARCUS AURELIUS
(as Caesar.)

MARCUS AURELIUS.
(as Emperor.)

FAUSTINA. (Junr.)

LUCILLA.

COMMODUS.

CRISPINA.

PERTINAX.

LVII.
TITIANA.

DIDIUS JULIANUS.

MANLIA   SCANTILLA.

DIDIA CLARA.

CLODIUS ALBINUS.

SEVERUS.

JULIA DOMNA.

CARACALLA.

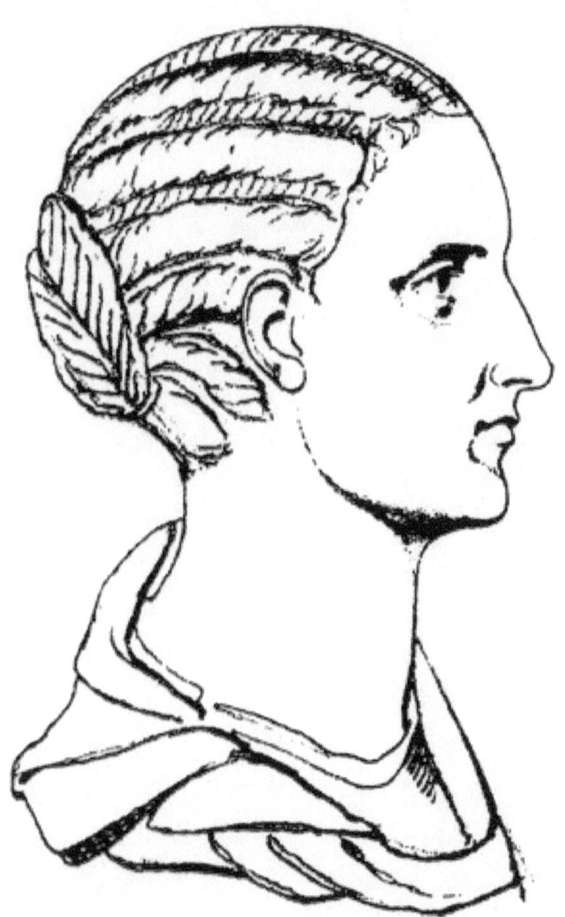

GETA.

MACRINUS.

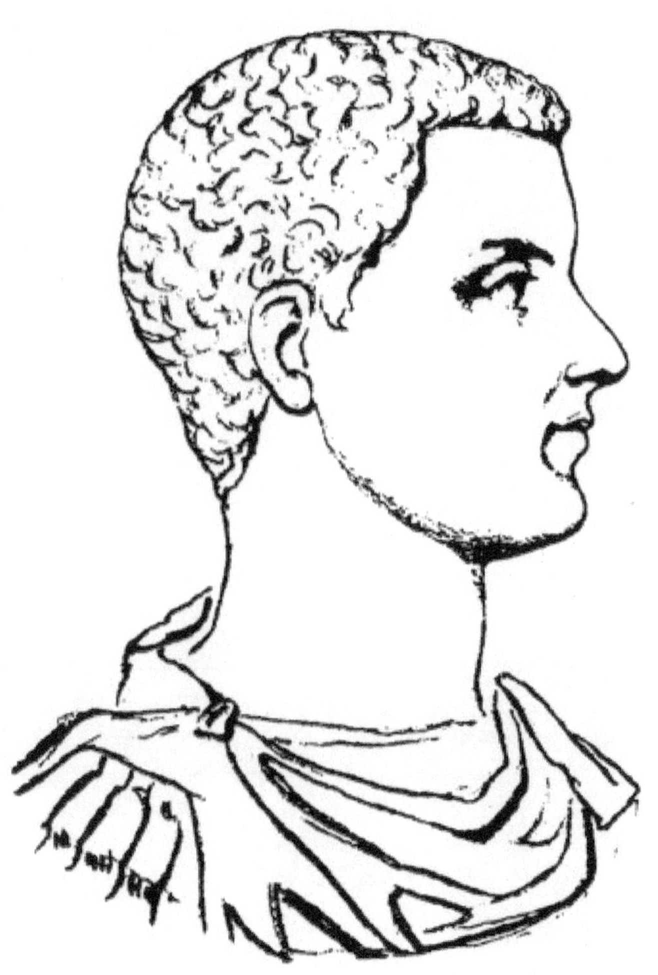

DIADUMENIANUS.

ELAGABALUS.

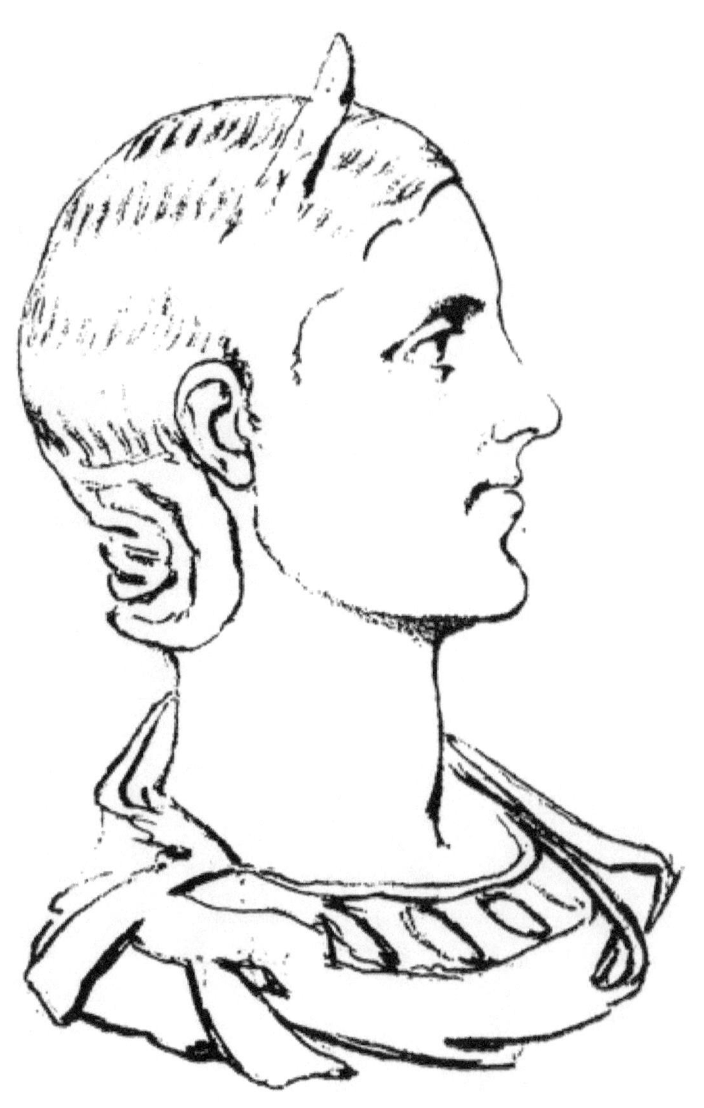

JULIA PAULA.

AQUILIA SEVERA.

ANNIA FAUSTINA.

JULIA SOAEMIAS.

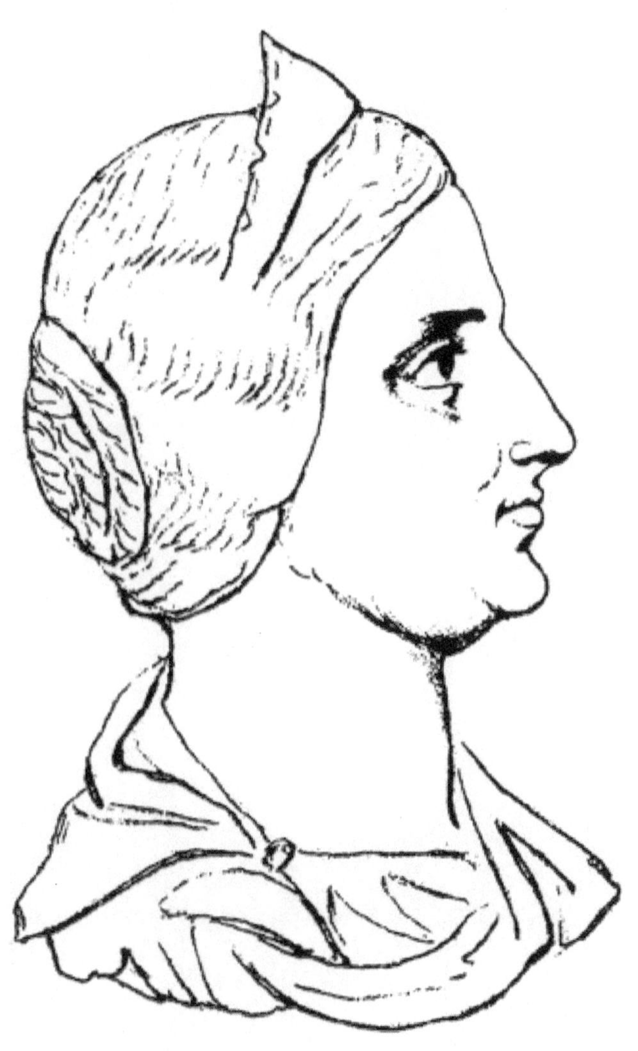

JULIA MAESA.

ALEXANDER SEVERUS.

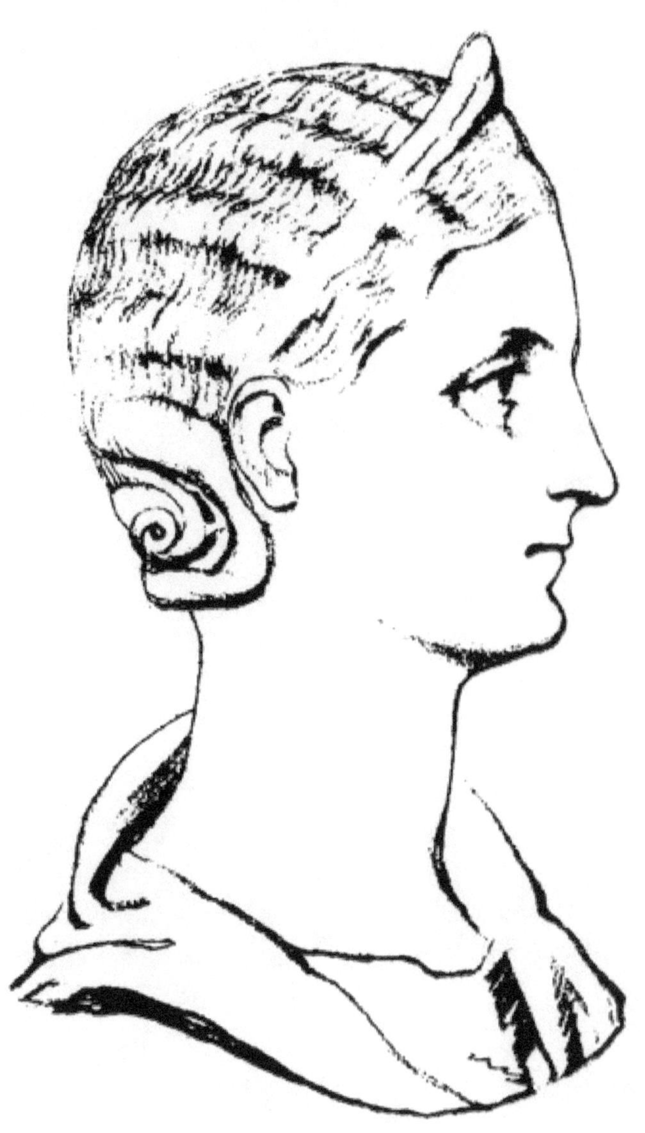

ORBIANA.

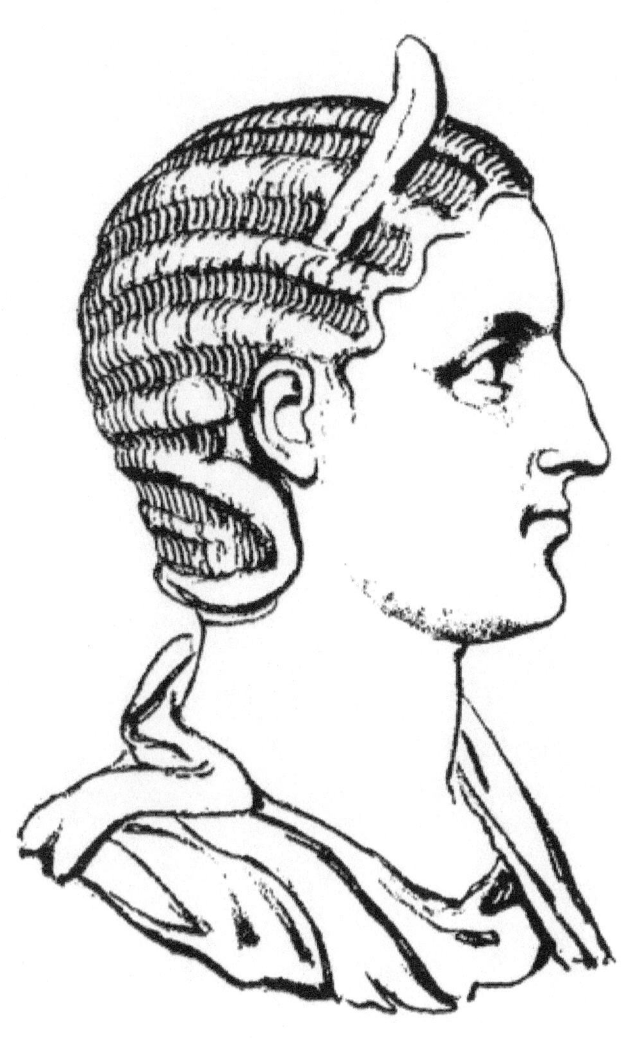

JULIA MAMAEA.

MAXIMINUS.

PAULINA.

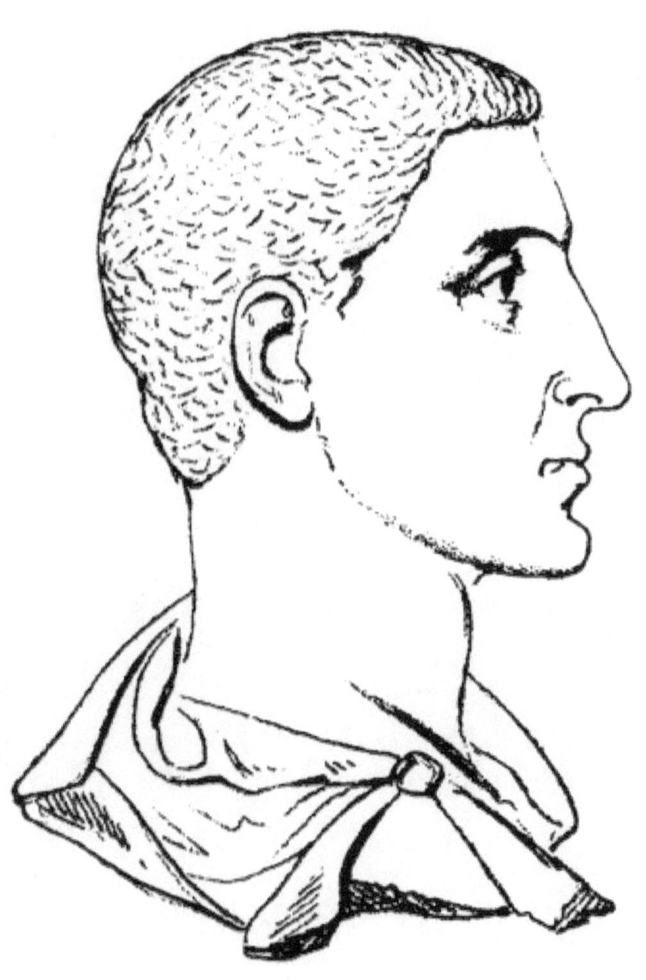

MAXIMUS CAESAR.

GORDIANUS AFRICANUS, I.

GORDIANUS AFRICANUS *(Jun.)*

BALBINUS.

PUPIENUS.

GORDIANUS PIUS.

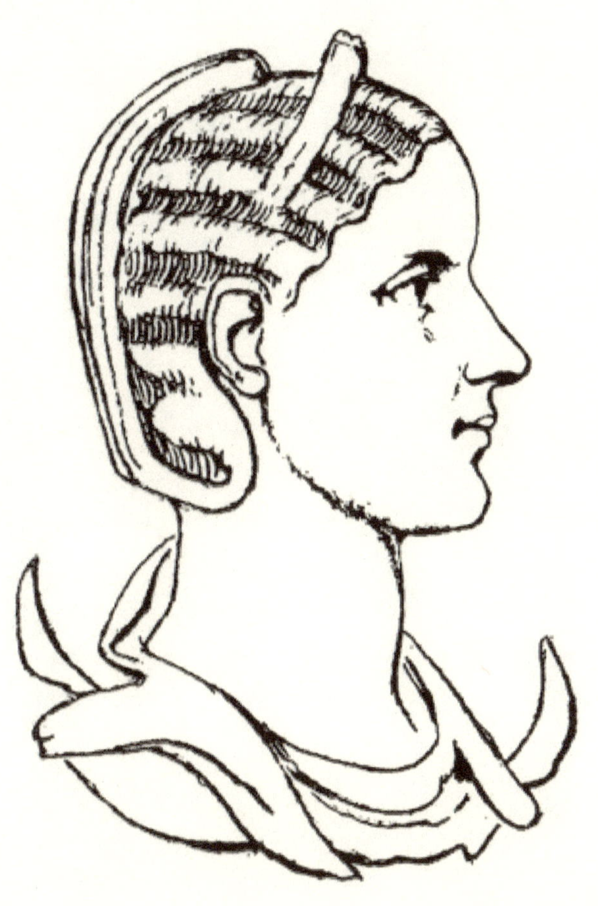

TRANQUILLINA.

PHILIPPUS (Sen.)

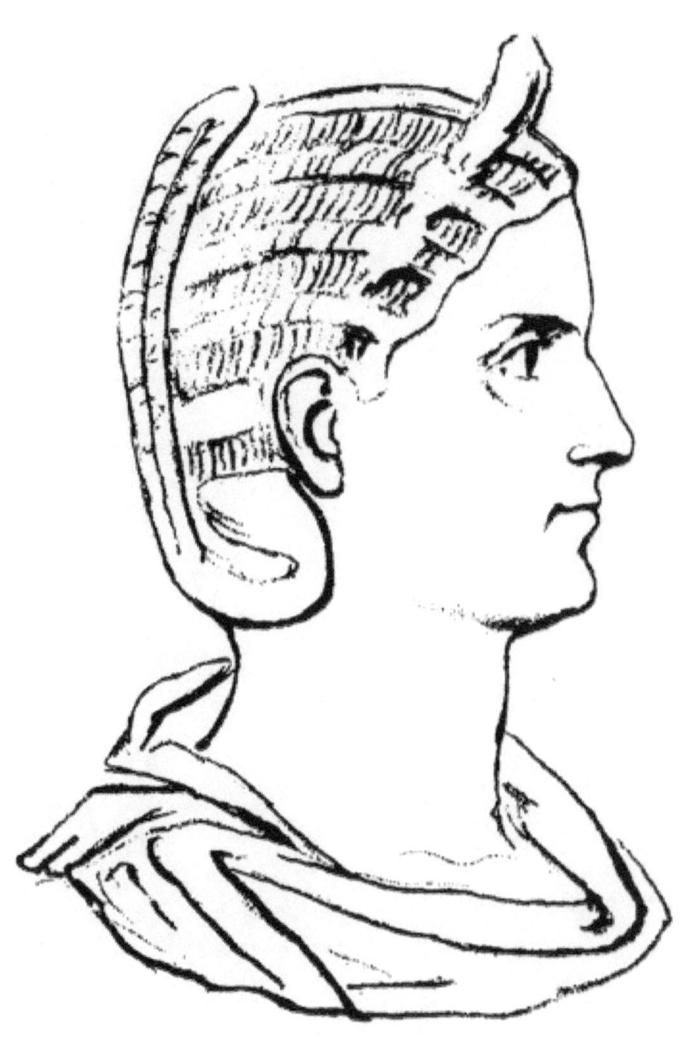

OTACILIA.

PHILIPPUS, *(Jun.)*

TRAJANUS DECIUS.

HERENNIUS ETRUSCUS.

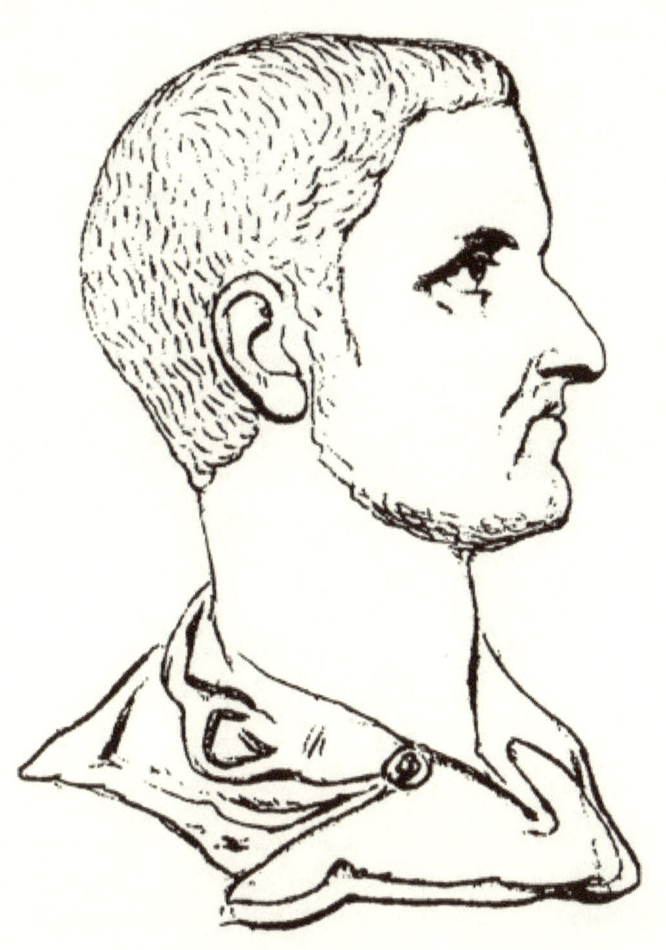

HOSTILIANUS.

TREBONIANUS GALLUS.

VOLUSIANUS.

XCVII.

AEMILIANUS.

VALERIANUS.

VALERIANUS. (No.2.)

MARINIANA.

C.

GALLIENUS.

POSTUMUS.

VICTORINUS.

MARIUS.

MARIUS.

TETRICUS. (Jun.r)

MACRIANUS.

CLAUDIUS GOTHICUS.

QUINTILLUS.

AURELIANUS.

CLAUDIUS COTHICUS.

AURELIANUS.

SEVERINA.

ZENOBIA.

VABALATHUS.

FLORIANUS.

PROBUS.

CARUS.

NUMERIANUS.

CARINUS.

MAGNIA URBICA.

CXXIV.

NIGRINIANUS.

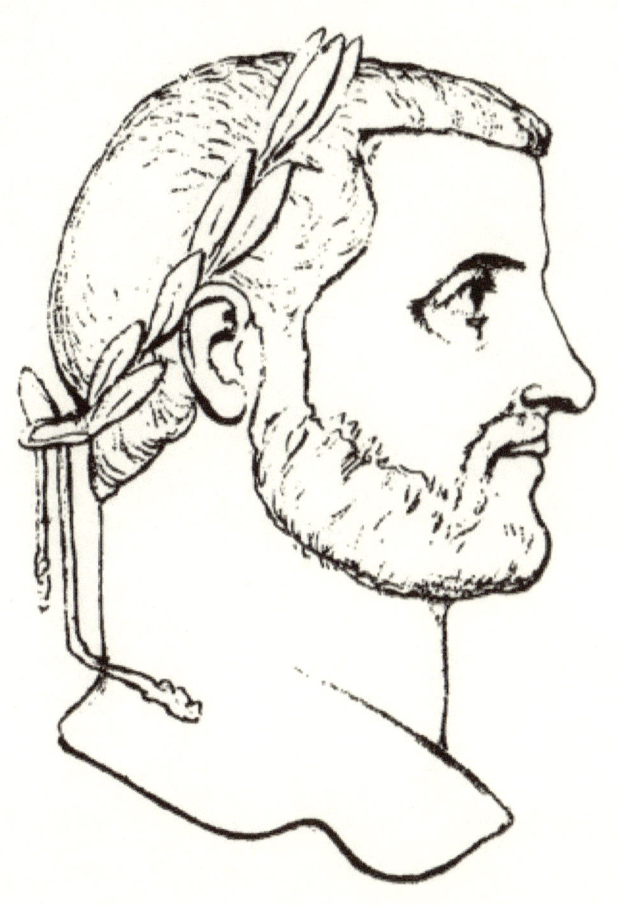

DIOCLETIANUS.

MAXIMIANUS HERCULEUS.

CARAUSIUS.

CONSTANTIUS CHLORUS.

HELENA.

THEODORA.

GALERIUS VALERIUS MAXIMIANUS.

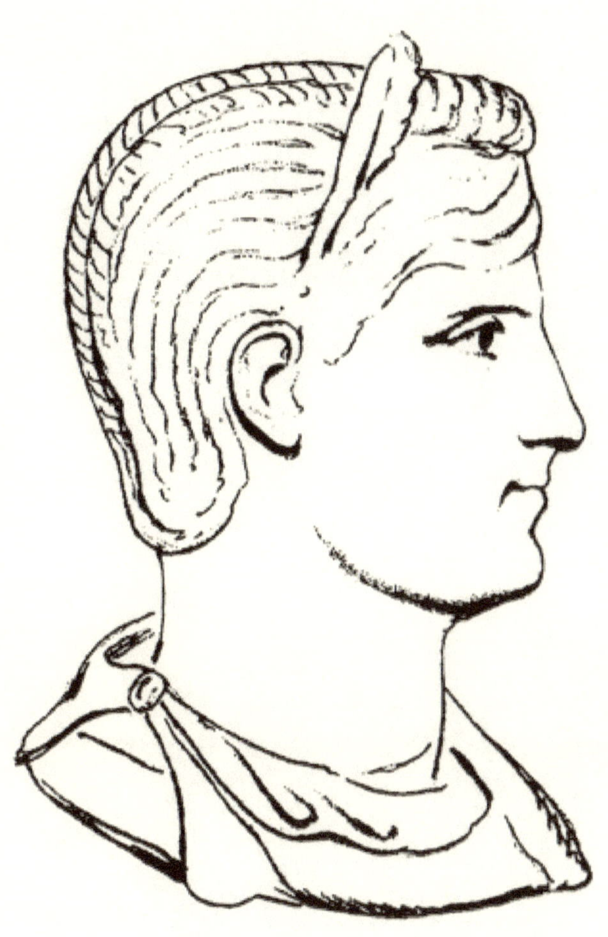

VALERIA.

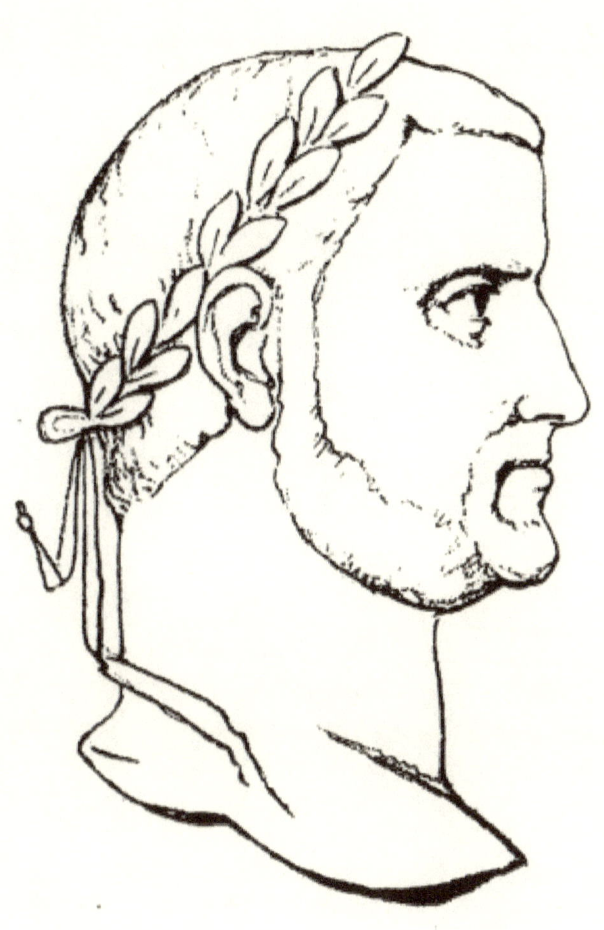

MAXIMINUS *(Daza)*

MAXENTIUS

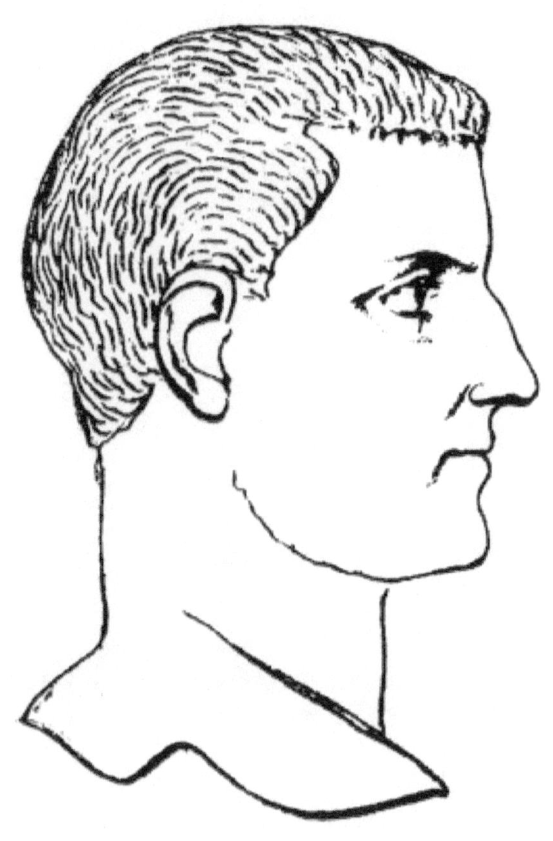

ROMULUS CAESAR.

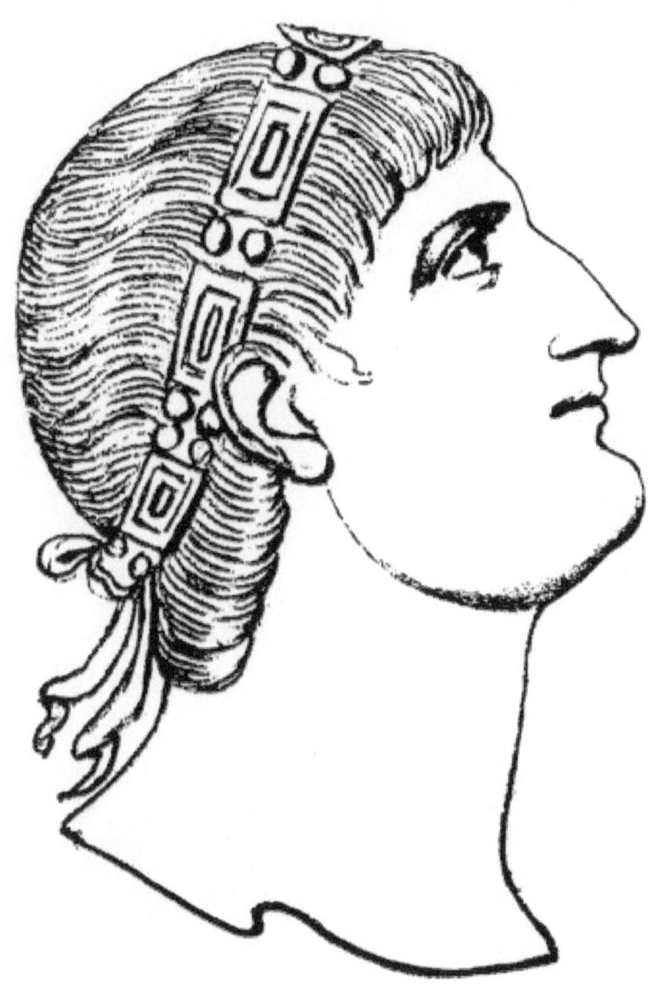

CONSTANTINUS MAXIMUS.

CONSTANTINUS MAXIMUS.

CONSTANTINUS MAXIMUS.

FAUSTA.

CRISPUS.

DELMATIUS.

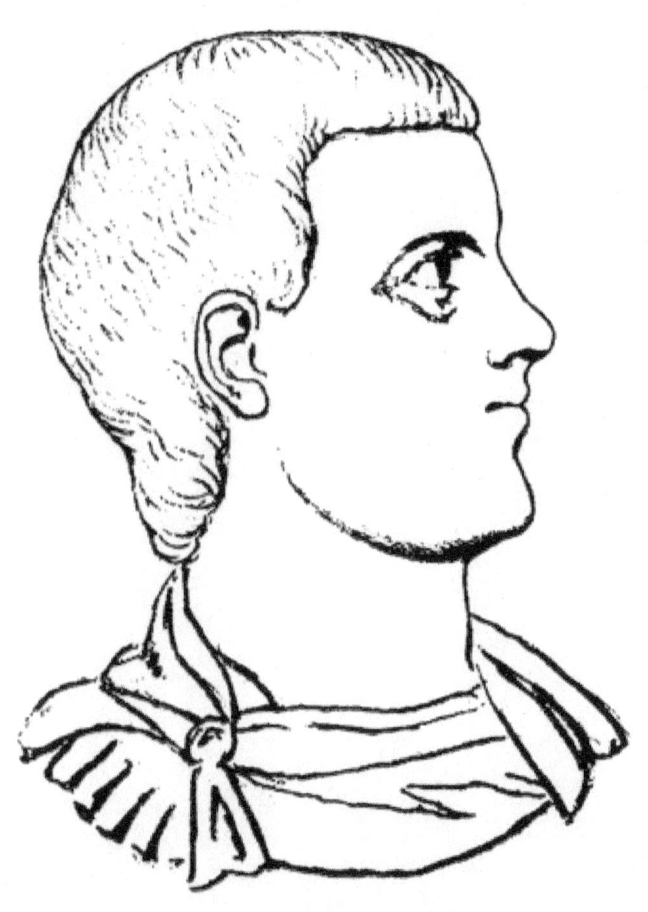

HANNIBALIANUS.

CONSTANTINUS. (Jun.)

CONSTANS.

CONSTANTIUS II.

CONSTANTIUS. II.

CONSTANTIUS, II.

FAUSTA. N.F.

NEPOTIANUS.

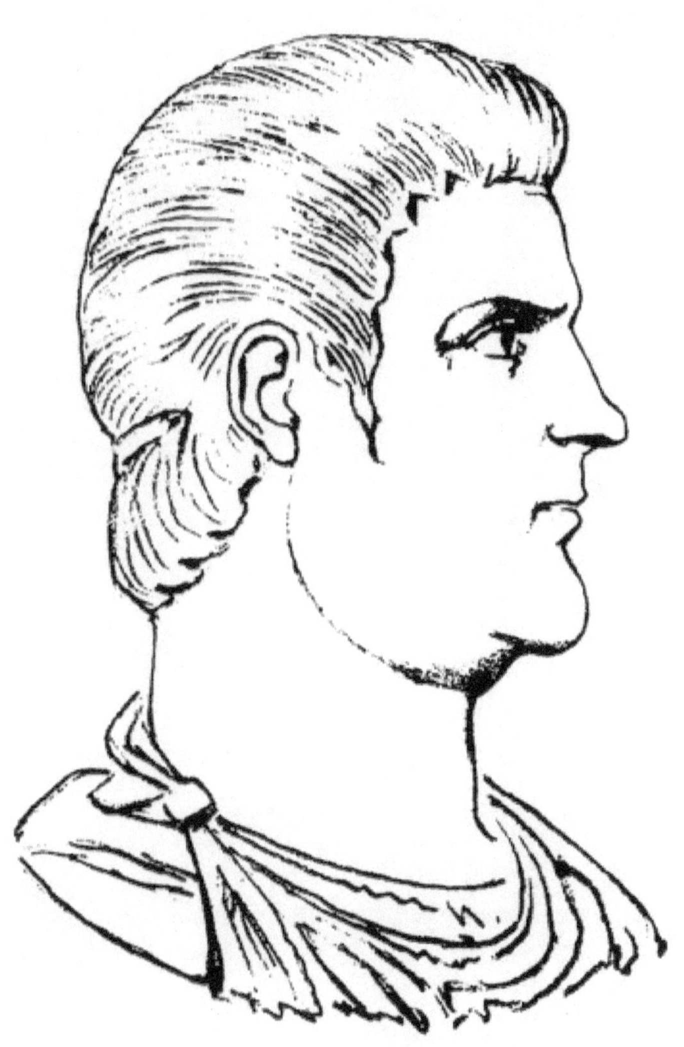

MAGNENTIUS.

DECENTIUS.

CONSTANTIUS GALLUS.

JULIANUS.
(as Caesar.)

JULIANUS II.
as Emperor.

JULIANUS AND HELENA.

(as Serapis and Isis.)

JULIANUS AND HELENA, *No.2.*
(as Serapis and Isis.)

HELENA. *(Juliani.)*

ROMULUS AUGUSTUS.